THE
Abaddon
Conspiracy

RAYMOND S. MOORE

THE Abaddon Conspiracy

BETHANY HOUSE PUBLISHERS
MINNEAPOLIS, MINNESOTA 55438
A Division of Bethany Fellowship, Inc.

Copyright © 1985
Raymond S. Moore
All Rights Reserved

Published by Bethany House Publishers
A Division of Bethany Fellowship, Inc.
6820 Auto Club Road, Minneapolis, Minnesota 55438

Printed in the United States of America

Library of Congress Cataloging in Publication Data

Moore, Raymond S.
   The Abaddon conspiracy.

   1. Devil. I. Title.
BT981.M66   1985   235   85-1438
ISBN 0-87123-825-X (pbk.)

"And they had a king over them, which is the angel of the bottomless pit, whose name in the Hebrew tongue is Abaddon," (Rev. 9:11).

RAYMOND S. MOORE holds an earned doctorate in Developmental Psychology and has been a Christian educator for fifty years. He has authored or contributed to many books by such publishers as Word Books, Thomas Nelson, Reader's Digest Press and others in the U.S. and abroad, and to many academic journals. Moore is the President of the Hewitt Research Foundation, headquartered in the state of Washington.

Contents

Prologue	9
1. Before the Beginning	11
2. Planting Ideas in the Garden	22
3. After Eden	29
4. Plans for the Family	37
5. The Threat of Enoch	44
6. Frustrations of a Flood	50
7. The Generation of the Unashamed	56
8. The Dividing of a Nation	62
9. Manipulating Israel	69
10. The Egyptian Fiasco	75
11. Substituting for the Government of God	80
12. The Babylonian Threat	88
13. The Strange Doings of Cyrus the Persian	96
14. The Grecian Syndrome	103
15. Confusion Concerning the Messiah	111
16. The Messiah's Disruption	117
17. The Roman Surrogate	125
18. The Darkest of the Ages	132
19. Renaissance and Reformation	139
20. The New Age	147

Prologue

Some time ago I became aware of a strange and terrible battle involving such strategy and intrigue that it stretched my imagination. It happened in a place astronomers have yet to discover. Bible writers called it heaven.

Long before earth's first flowers bloomed, this war exploded, started by Lucifer. Its fallout infected the whole universe, particularly our small and now shadowed planet. This war has raged for at least six thousand years, or longer.

I realize that this story seems strange, like something out of science fiction. Yet it is true. It began in the heavens, by Lucifer's choice; it later centered on earth. Eventually, I am told, it will be finished here.

This war represented no ordinary conflict, for the first battle involved the Deity—heaven's joint Commanders—and the highest generals in heaven.

Making inquiry, I eventually pieced the story together from a symphony of sources, including the new chief of staff of heaven's forces, Gabriel, the archangel of God. Gabriel, whose name means "man of God," replaced the rebel general, Lucifer.

This is essentially the account I learned from Gabriel and the record keepers. Although appearing stranger than fiction, the brief record presented here is absolutely true, for the recorders actually lived through all the events. They listened to their enemy, and their retelling of Lucifer's lectures to his angels clings as closely to fact as our tape recordings of today. Though many told me the story, for simplicity's sake I present it here as a conversation between Gabriel and me.

1
BEFORE THE BEGINNING

"How," I demanded, "could war start in a perfect society? What breeds war? Isn't it poverty or covetousness or fear?"

"Eons before the earth was formed," Gabriel began, "my home was the scene of festive meetings. There, as Job put it, the morning stars sang together and the sons of God shouted for joy. The corporate heads of heaven were the Father, Son and Holy Spirit."

"Where did they come from?" I wondered aloud.

"Of their beginnings," said Gabriel, "no creature understands. The holy Three of the Godhead are eternal—no beginning and no end. All creation accepted this fact, for to understand the Godhead was impossible for them. How can a flea understand a dog? How can a dog know a man? How can a man fully comprehend God? These Three are eternal, infinitely greater than the rest of us. Not only were they before all things, but in them all things are held together. We had an implicit obedience that grew out of reverence and love. Yet we hardly knew that we obeyed; we simply followed our Leader's example of love."

"You refer to all of the Godhead as eternal?" I interrupted.

"Yes," said Gabriel, "and as I tell this story it is important that we keep details clear and simple. When I speak of God, I refer to the Godhead, otherwise called the Deity, or the Trinity—the eternal Three. I will refer to the Father, the Son (or

Christ as He was named on earth), and the Holy Spirit by name.

"From the edge of time, the organization of heaven was one of perfect order. All but the Deity were creatures—created by our loving God. Each of us fully accepted the extent of his own responsibility and the limits of his own authority.

"In the throne room of heaven, there served an angel whose wisdom and authority ranged above all others, one who stood among the ceaseless beams of glory which surrounded our eternal Father. We loved, honored and reverenced him as the special representative of the Most High. We were delighted to carry out his commands, for he perfectly reflected the nature of the Creator.

"It was his privilege to reveal God's purpose to the universe, and when he mounted the golden podium to direct our choir, his glorious voice soared above all the other angels in melody given by God."

"But who was this angel?" I asked impatiently.

Gabriel spoke softly. "His name was Lucifer, Son of the Morning. Dwelling in the light of the Father's presence, this seraph prince realized the power he held over all the other angels."

"A colossal ego!"

"Oh, no. He was totally responsible and completely reverent toward God. And he not only cheerfully obeyed his every command, but sensed his close ties to the Son of God.

"A brilliant individual, Lucifer, and the keeper of God's wisdom. Impossible," Gabriel added, "for you to comprehend. And an exceedingly handsome angel. Perhaps his close association with the Father gave his face an added dimension of love and joy. As the prophet Ezekiel said, he was 'full of wisdom and perfect in beauty.'"

"Then how," I demanded, "could he possibly become an enemy?"

"You see," Gabriel explained, "the character of the Trinity is fondly expressed in their determination to share every possible quality and power with all creation. The key is the gift of choice—a frightening power to choose for ourselves, whether for or against our Creator. Yet without this gift we could not know the highest joy of loyalty and obedience and Godlike love. We would be little more than automatons or slaves."

"You mean that any of you could, in fact, rebel?"

He nodded. "The Godhead took an immense risk that some of us might turn against them. Yet they gave us this awesome gift. So we did not obey as robots or slaves, but rather from a deep gratitude, reverence and affection for God.

"To us, home was as it still is today, a city built with jewels and paved with transparent gold. It is watered by the River of God and lighted by His presence. But more important than all that was our freedom—without the illness, sorrow and death that you know—to share the wonders of the universe."

I listened, bewildered, silently comparing Gabriel's home with the world I knew.

"On one occasion," he continued, "the Trinity announced their plan to create a new order of being. They said they would call him 'man.' And they would prepare a planet for him. He would possess the same power of choice as we, that he might also know the fullness of divine loyalty and love. And he would reproduce himself in the image of God.

"The Son first told us the news," said Gabriel. "By agreement with the Trinity, He would be the Creator of man. He described how we would be the guardians of the new race."

"Exciting news," I murmured. "I cannot really imagine it."

"Yes, but it also raised questions such as we had never before known—dark, ugly questions. For the first time, apparently, Lucifer seemed to think more of himself than of God. He wondered out loud why they had not counseled with him—the loftiest of all angels—for this unique creation. He wondered why the Son should direct such creation instead of him, the archangel. He seemed to forget that he was a creature, not the Creator. Instead of love, he cherished thoughts of envy. As he contemplated the plan, he found himself gripped by jealousy, even hatred, of the Son of God. Choosing against God!"

"But that seems unlikely in a perfect environment," I protested.

"Yet, true." Gabriel said sadly. "He had the power of choice."

He read the lingering uncertainty in my eyes.

"You see, as the Son of the Morning began to lose the sense of his creaturehood," Gabriel pointed out, "he pushed into the back of his mind the fact that the Son of God is eternal, divine, and one of the Three to whom he, Lucifer, owed his creation, his very life."

"But that," I said, "is the way with sin—it is self-deceiving."

"Yes, discord was utterly new in heaven, so Christ, the Son, patiently tried to reason with Lucifer. But his choice grew against God. Like darkness overtaking the day, our angel leader became centered in himself, and before long he began to confide his doubts and ambitions to those closest to him. I was one of them.

"Some of them listened, and to those he told more. Yet most of us turned away in uncertainty and deep concern. As he scheduled the duties of the angels, a strange new partiality soon became apparent to us. He insisted that we were pawns of an arbitrary despot."

Silently I listened, astonished at this story of bold defiance before the throne of God.

"Many who had been close to Lucifer pleaded that he change his course," continued Gabriel. "I remember his apparent hypocrisy at our choir sessions. He smiled. He sang. We wondered . . . has he changed? But he had not; he still whispered his unhappiness around heaven.

"As he used lies, half-truths and insinuations as weapons, we saw the harmony of heaven begin to shatter." Pain filled Gabriel's eyes. "Our Father tried. Oh, how He tried. But Lucifer enjoyed his cunning; while he claimed loyalty to God, he urged that changes in the laws of heaven were necessary. He demanded equality with the Son, the Creator himself."

"A created being?" I gasped. "Equality with God?"

"Yes, he moved from angel to angel, repeating and twisting our words, pitting us against each other. Finally God summoned him to a carefully structured meeting of most solemn warnings and cautions. The words of the Trinity were well-reasoned. They later told how they reminded Lucifer of his beginnings and how he owed his very life to them. They repeated the story of his exaltation to the highest creature office and pointed out his eternal loss if he did not change."

Gabriel paused, adding almost to himself. "Oh, how God yearned over Lucifer. How He loved him!"

"And still Lucifer turned against Him?" I asked incredulously.

Gabriel nodded with obvious anguish.

I could not understand. "That's insane!" I cried.

"Exactly," he replied. "Sin is like that. It is without reason—no reason at all for its beginnings."

Already my head ached as my mind stretched to believe.

Then Gabriel continued. "After he talked with the Godhead, Lucifer seemed stirred. I understand that he bowed low in apparent reverence and adoration to Christ. But the seeds of unrest were already sown. When he returned to those angels he had tempted and persuaded, they asked him hard questions, about change, a possible shift of his loyalties back to God. He felt trapped and feared his followers might think him weak.

"Too proud for his own good, he renewed his desire to be not only above all other angels but also to be equal with Christ. The angels' confidence in his leadership, he reasoned, would be destroyed if he turned back now.

"Can you picture him conferring with his followers?" Gabriel asked me. "Can you see the mask of certainty he wears to cover his fear? 'I have not changed my position,' he asserted. 'The laws of heaven must change.'

"Then he redoubled his efforts to recruit as many angels as possible for his purposes. He worked vigorously and cleverly to win us. Everything simple he clouded with mystery in order to cast doubt on the plainest statements of God. He flattered those who stopped to consider his viewpoint. He worked behind the scenes. Heaven had never known such a spectacle, and even as it happened, many of us found it hard to believe." Gabriel's words came slowly. "One-third of my comrades chose to turn from our Father and follow Lucifer."

"He turned totally away from God?"

"He did. His obsessive jealousy of the Son became starkly obvious to us who remained loyal to God. We were frightened of him, and that fear—a new emotion to us—lay heavily on us. We feared his ability to twist words, to make the simple complex and the innocent vile. Our reasoning seemed irrational to him when viewed from his pedestal.

"Regardless of pleas and warnings, he determined to spread discontent throughout heaven and ultimately to assume the very command of Christ. This required a conscious decision to rebel against our long-suffering Father."

"But," I cried, "couldn't the Father somehow clear Lucifer's mind? Is He not all-powerful?"

"Remember," Gabriel reminded me kindly but firmly, "the Father guaranteed us the right of choice. We are creatures of reason and can evaluate the likely results of our choices. The Father bore long with Lucifer, much longer than we ever thought He dared. But Lucifer interpreted this patience as weakness. He confused popularity with power, and so convinced himself that his popularity and influence exceeded even that of the Son that he flouted the authority of heaven by assembling angels to hear his claims. We were astounded and horrified. Our leader, Lucifer, had been a channel of God's power for so long that we found his deceiving himself into believing himself equal to the Source of that power a mystery."

"It sounds like so many of us here on earth," I mused.

"Indeed," Gabriel agreed. "Unfortunate, but true. Next," he continued, "Lucifer vowed, 'I will exalt my throne above the stars of God. . . . I will be like the Most High.' By then he had become so skilled in placing truth within a framework of error that it appeared he actually could not tell the difference."

I shook my head; my mind was a tangle of might-have-beens.

"So to us who remained loyal, the lines were sharply drawn. Lucifer's once quiet deception had ripened into bold and active revolt. We tried earnestly, even desperately, to reconcile him with the Son and with God's laws. For millenniums he had happily obeyed out of the certainty that obedience brought security and joy. We reminded him that God's laws were laws of love, pointing out that before he began his rebellion, we didn't even realize God had laws. We merely acted in response to His love.

"He would not listen. Indeed, he had gone past the point of no return. Then open conflict erupted, shattering the serenity of heaven."

"War?"

"War," Gabriel said. "Unspeakable, unthinkable, but true. Heaven watched in fear and amazement as the Trinity called for a decision. They asked us to speak up for or against the Divine Law, including a pledge of loyalty to the Holy Three. 'There must be no hesitancy or equivocation,' they said, reminding us that the laws of God—the rules of heaven—were established in love for the protection of His creation much as you, on earth, build a guardrail at the edge of an oft-visited cliff. 'Your decision will be final,' they told us. 'All who choose against God will have to leave heaven.' "

"Just like that?"

"Yes. They spoke kindly but simply. Their message was absolutely clear—and absolutely final."

A wave of sorrow washed over me as I wondered how God had endured such grief.

"We who were loyal dreaded this finality, but we welcomed its relief from the terror Lucifer had brought. We had been astonished at the forbearance of the Godhead and yearned again for the peace we had enjoyed."

Gabriel hesitated. "What happened?" I pled anxiously.

"Lucifer's followers became so confident of their wisdom and power that they broke out in open warfare against us. We saw their faces change, expressing hatred and disgust. They fought viciously and skillfully against us who were loyal to God.

"Then in the midst of the fighting, the Father expelled Lucifer and his followers—a third of all the angels—from their home. With one gigantic gesture, as if His great hand was brushing them away, God cast them from heaven."

"Why didn't He just destroy them?" I asked.

"The Deity knew that there might be lingering doubts even among those who were loyal," Gabriel replied. "And they knew that many of us would mourn the loss of the fallen angels. Even their war against us did not erase the millions of joyful memories of the eons we had shared.

"So Infinite Wisdom decided that Lucifer and his followers must be allowed to demonstrate the true character of their rebellion, leaving no vestige of doubt in the minds of any creature. And this decision carried with it an unspeakable possibility: the risk of eternal disruption of the universe!"

Gabriel must have seen alarm in my eyes.

"You will understand this more clearly," he assured me, "as we tell you of Lucifer's lectures to his angels and report the events of the centuries. In a sense, it was satisfying to us that the Father swept them like lightning out of heaven. Yet strange regrets lingered in our minds. God understood. The Deity promised us that the tangle of questions would eventually become unsnarled. With great compassion, they also assured us that none of the rebels—except Lucifer—would be allowed to return. For a limited time he could represent himself as the master of the new world in the councils of the universe—until the Redeemer reclaimed His sovereignty."

"Actually to be an advisor to God?" I asked.

"Yes, in the sense that he later became ruler of your world. However, he could no longer be called Lucifer in heaven, for with his expulsion the Light Bearer, the Morning Star, was renamed 'Satan'—the 'accuser,' 'the devil.'

"At this point," Gabriel said simply, "God appointed me to Lucifer's place."

"As the archangel?"

"Yes. Then the Godhead told us they had agreed on a plan which would permit Lucifer, now Satan, and his rebellious followers freedom to disrupt the world. No question must remain in the minds of the Deity's loyal creatures about their wisdom, fairness and love. The inhabitants of the yet uncreated earth would be given a fair but crucial test.

"If Satan somehow succeeded in deceiving mankind, then that would establish his claim to kingship of the world, and Divinity's ultimate sacrifice would be made. The Son—the Creator himself—would come to the world and would live and walk among them as true man. He would submit to whatever grueling inquisition and cruelty the deceiver could devise. Only when—and *if*—He survived these temptations without the slightest capitulation in thought, word or act would Satan's defeat be insured."

"Could there be no other solution?" I wondered.

"No, this only; nothing less could verify God's throne as an office of love and set an eternal example before all creation."

"Not even an angel?"

"Hardly. Only the Creator could redeem. He could not possibly pass His accountability to a created being.

"In due time the Son created the new world, simply and efficiently as the Scriptures record. The new creation centered on a 'Garden of Eden' in which were placed a man and a woman, Adam and Eve, to rule under the guidance of God. But in that garden God placed one tree off-limits to the new and perfect pair. The testing ground of the fledging world, its fruit was not to be eaten by Adam and Eve. 'If you eat of the fruit of this tree,' God told them, 'you will surely die.' "

"Just this one tree?"

"Yes. Do you think you could have devised a simpler, clearer test?"

I could think of none.

"Christ carefully admonished them to stay away from this tree. If they obeyed His simple instructions, all of Satan's sophistries would have no power against them. It was a matter of choice. The Creator made certain that Adam and Eve were carefully cued as to Satan's methods. I know, for I was one of those who outlined Satan's revolt and warned that he would try to seize their loyalty. But despite the Creator's careful explanation, the woman and man reacted in disobedience.

"Satan knew that if he could entice the youthful pair to take his word over God's, he could set the stage for the possible fall of the Son himself. And if in any wily way he could induce the Son to violate the law of God in the slightest iota, then the devil of devils could laugh forevermore in the face of God."

"An utterly exhausting thought," came my reaction. And Gabriel spoke as though his thoughts were mine.

"Convinced that deceit and cunning would succeed where force had failed in heaven, Satan began to train his angels carefully. He summoned them to a series of seminars, or councils. To them he was still Lucifer, the Light Bearer, Son of the Morning, and still determined to be like the Most High. If he could not move up with God, he determined to bring God down with him. Adam and Eve were only pawns in his battle against Deity, and in that war his defiance knew no bounds.

"Bear in mind that Satan and his demons are superhuman. They have the ability to be visible or invisible, to appear and to disappear, and to perform apparently Godlike miracles. Their meetings were sometimes held at Satan's central headquarters, sometimes elsewhere behind mysterious veils of darkness for which he is so well-known. Sometimes he summoned all his followers; sometimes he met with his key officers alone."

I wondered aloud how Satan worked, and asked to know the end of things, lest I were beguiled like Adam and Eve and Satan's angels.

"I would like to tell you the final outcome of this—which we now know well," Gabriel smiled, "but I must save that. First I will show you how Lucifer operates. But I do this, remember, not to devote your mind to Satan, but to show you how love found a way to deal with him—through the Son.

"The first of his talks centered on Eden and the happy couple who tended God's garden there. Our intelligence forces monitored Satan's every planning session, every demon instruction. Although his lectures are in abridged form, I have time to give you only a few of the key ones now—enough that you can better understand his almost infinite capacity for deception and the kind of plans he may have for you."

A tingle of fear ran down my spine.

"His lectures will reveal your vulnerability," he said, "which is much greater than you think . . . certainly greater than Eve or Adam first imagined. You will find that Satan grew even more skilled at placing truth in a bed of error.

"We will use visual aids from heaven's vaults to compress centuries into minutes. I will largely omit the many regional staff sessions under his lower commands. You understand, of course, that with such superhuman individuals as Satan, time is quickly consumed: a century is short-term. And to avoid confusion, since his own fallen angels (demons) are involved and they still call him Lucifer, I will use that name in reciting his lectures to you."

My anticipation was a strange combination of eagerness and dread, of euphoria and exhaustion.

Very quickly Gabriel threw the picture onto a huge screen. The panorama was in such color as I had never before seen. And there was Lucifer . . .

2
PLANTING IDEAS IN THE GARDEN

"I want you to understand," Lucifer began, "that this is a historic occasion—a crucial council of the universe." He looked over the vast audience before him. Their once handsome faces were now shadowed by anger, hate and—fear. Superhuman, their eyes perceived him as if he were at their sides. They held the face of Lucifer, silently begging him for reassurance that the path they'd chosen would bring them good. He leaned forward, his words ringing.

"There is no unity like ours; there are no higher goals. We are instituting our plan and purpose of turning man against himself and his Maker, and humbling the Son, our enemy, who holds himself above us all. We will bring down the kingdom of God.

"First, I lay before you our foundation principles." His strong hands, long fingers clutched the podium. "Gaining control of earth justifies any means, and all my rules are to be implicitly obeyed." His eyes locked on Nabal, his deputy. "There will be no exceptions.

"In following me you surrendered all choice. I have made my choice. You have made yours. You can't go back. Heaven is now closed to us. We have no alternative but to deny the inhabitants of earth the free access to God we once had. We will prove Him to be severe and unforgiving by portraying Him as a creature of hate, a rigid, arbitrary, relentless Spirit who eagerly awaits the slightest error as an excuse to torment or punish those He has created. I am your god; you will look to me."

He continued to speak hypnotically. "We will counter His every ploy, obstruct every device He cherishes and counterfeit every principle He holds dear. These forgeries shall be clever enough to deceive even those closest to Him. We must persuade His people to trust in their own reason more than in any instruction He might give them. By appealing to their pride—and, oh, they'll have pride—we can insure that they are consumed with themselves.

"Our long-range plan takes many forms. It begins with bringing death to the earth, and when that is accomplished we shall frequently impersonate those who have died. By appearing as angels of God, our work will be interpreted by these people as acts of God. Thus confusing them, we can create many substitutes for what God calls His truths. Indeed, I have plans for the most subtle impersonations of the angels and even the Godhead itself, particularly the Son and Holy Spirit."

He stood straight, his words coming fast and clipped. "Ours is a military organization. Understand this once and for all: *We are at war with God.* Oh, you may offer counsel, but you must unfailingly follow the established channels through your commanders. On all matters of policy my word is final. I expect *total* loyalty, *total* obedience. You have no other choice."

"We hear you well," echoed his deputy Nabal, and the demons roared with applause.

Lucifer paused, momentarily distracted but deep in thought.

"The weakness of the Father should be obvious. His fear of me is so great that He is compelled to accept my participation in His divine councils. They still let me into heaven, you know; they don't dare keep me out. While we have lost the first battle, we have not lost the war.

"We have now witnessed the Son's creation of the new world. This is the Father's pride and joy; and the new couple, His delight." A strange, almost sad expression crossed his face.

"At any rate, Christ has given them His little test which I will soon represent as absurd. I speak, of course, of the tree of the knowledge of good and evil. He is compelled to allow us there, and this will be His death knell. We will conquer Him on His own soil—in the Garden of Eden. The new favored world will become our kingdom, the garden our home. Then we will control the tree of life, and our future will be insured. The first test is of such great consequence that I will personally carry out the attack. I have already worked out a plan." He licked his lips.

Raa, whose name meant "evil," stood momentarily as if to demonstrate the importance of dialogue from them all. "Please make it clear that this plan was devised by the entire staff."

"Indeed," Lucifer acknowledged, then quickly continued: "Christ has fully warned the young couple about our probable strategy. No doubt God's angels will also admonish them. I shall see that those warnings appear ominous, rather than as messages of love. My spirit, my influence, like that of the Holy Spirit, is pervasive down here. My plan is to continually work to raise questions in their minds concerning the Son's admonitions."

The group leaned forward, eager to hear his plan.

"First, I will concentrate on the woman. Since Adam is the head of the garden and strongly feels his responsibility, Eve will be more vulnerable. Eventually I intend to draw her to the forbidden tree by lilting songs of birds, unusual colors in the sunlight, and a sense of independence. But I won't approach her in person. That would be too obvious and that could frighten her. Remember, always avoid confrontations until you are certain you have the situation in hand.

"Ultimately I will approach her through the most beautiful creature in the garden. I've been watching her and have observed that she is intrigued with the great serpent—the largest one in Eden—its brilliant colors and its transluscent wings. I will use him, the creature she so highly regards. Day by day he will carefully draw her from tree to tree, closer and closer to the forbidden tree—always when her husband is elsewhere in the garden. We must keep him as far as possible from her side. And he must become more and more comfortable in her independence and solitude. Certain ones of you are to assist in distracting the man while I entice the woman to the tree. She will come to trust in herself more than in God, even in doing His work in the garden. Thus we will plant the first seed of rebellion which shall flourish and abound throughout the ages."

"But surely God has put angels at their sides," called out Lashan.

"Lashan, you are well named," said Lucifer cynically to the demon whose name meant "tongue." "However, you have no need to concern your sharp mind. Once Eve reaches the forbidden tree, she is in my control. God allows her to choose. Even our enemies can't prevent that.

"Don't worry, Lashan. I'll speak gently. I have been watching her closely and know her better than she knows herself."

Across the vast assembly, heads nodded.

"My voice will be well-modulated and reassuring. First, I'll speak of her beauty; she *is* lovely in a naive sort of way. It should be easy enough to reach the vanity hidden under that beautiful hair.

"Speaking through the serpent, I will tell her that I have new things for her to learn. Wisdom, for example—a secret wisdom known only by the gods. *My* great wisdom.

"Oh, she will talk to me. Probably a bit hesitantly at first, but I daresay she'll loosen up in time. Reason with her is sure to work." He was rambling now, talking as much to himself as to his audience. "She has pride; everyone has pride—the kind that tears God's creatures to pieces." He smiled. "Almost a pity for one so newly-formed, and yet our survival depends upon it."

Nabal jerked Lucifer up with another sharp reminder. "Please explain exactly *how* as well as *what* you plan to do."

Lucifer drew himself up. "She must be made to wish to excel, to learn more than God has told her, to experience more than He allows. And I'll entice her with the delicacies God withholds. Oh, the fruit cf that tree, to be sure—but far more. Wisdom. To know as much as I. To know as much as God.

"He doesn't call it the tree of the knowledge of good and evil for naught." A dry, mirthless laugh shook his large shoulders. "She knows good. I will teach her evil. I will persuade her that in reality God is daring her to disobey."

In the audience Ebed, another of Lucifer's followers, unthinkingly yawned. Lucifer's eyes narrowed; he directed his words to the one named "slavery." "I will lead Eve to view me as a myth, unreal. God speaks to her of Satan—the enemy. I'll teach her that that enemy is only a figment of the imagination of a paranoid God.

"The secret lies in gaining her trust. Within minutes, I will be her confidante and friend. Once she's excited at the possibilities of secret knowledge, she can be enchanted with the prospect of being a princess in my kingdom rather than a slave in God's. Don't forget, God's demands are absolute.

"So are mine, but she will not know.

"Through my clever leading, she'll develop a passion for the unknown which she'll pass to her children and grandchildren, *ad infinitum.*

"I will, in my own subtle way, dare her to learn good *and* evil. Once she accepts my dare, she must forever do my bidding."

He stopped, grinning, waiting for the applause that grew, swelling and thundering, until he raised his hands for silence. "Thank you. Thank you. You have wisely chosen your god. We will prevail!

"Then," he continued, "I will leave her in the care of a selected few of you, while I deal with the man. I will interrupt Adam's preoccupation—thanks to you, comrades—and then obsess him with panic. Suddenly the garden shall seem alien to him as he rushes wildly about, searching for his wife.

"He will find her soon enough, but will be unprepared for the new light of wisdom—*my* wisdom—in her eyes.

"Picture him, comrades, God's perfect man, startled to the brink of insanity. I plan to twist his mind until he feels forced to work out his own solution instead of turning, questioning, to God. I know Adam's weaknesses. First, he'll remonstrate with her for straying away, but then he'll look again and suddenly see what she's become. He'll see the excitement in her eyes and the pout I will give her lips. Perhaps she'll even cry"—Lucifer's laughter rang out—"the first tears on earth, if you do not count your own.

"Confused, Adam will be susceptible to my temptations." Lucifer paused. "Temptation: a key word for you. Has a nice sound, don't you think? You can twist or corrupt God's commands in their minds, and make our way desirable.

"Getting back to Adam, watch me tear him with doubts about God in his sympathy and love for Eve. Surely his first thought will be to turn to God, for that is his nature now. But by suggesting that he can keep Eve only by sharing her new wisdom, he can be pushed to despair.

"He'll be reluctant, but never fear—he'll eat from her hand."

Ariun, the demon of "cunning," winked. "And then?"

"Then he will be stricken with guilt as he realizes the awesomeness of defying God. In this state he'll turn away from Eve. As I remind him that God charged him with her protection, anger will boil within him against his pretty bride. Anger and guilt will destroy every rational thought, and in that moment he might even hate her.

"Then Adam will look at her again with an accompanying astonishing change. Their eyes will meet, then drop, then turn away, for they shall be ashamed in their nakedness."

Wide smiles pervaded the assembly, elbows nudged one another, laughter roared from the audience. Lucifer bowed. "Their guilt is to be compounded by more new emotions—terror and remorse. Wisdom also, for the two. The knowledge of good *and* evil."

His voice grew softer. "At that time we must bring them completely into our fellowship. If I know the Godhead, they'll have a grandiose scheme to retrieve them, but we must work to convince Adam and Eve that their greatest security lies with us. They must believe that they are prince and princess in this earthly kingdom which we will then control. It is of utmost importance that we secure their loyalty. They must be made to believe that God will be vicious in His retribution and gleeful that He caught them in the act of violating His absurd conditions.

"Again, watch me closely and learn from my wisdom. Each of you are at the disposal of your commanders who are strictly accountable to me. There will be no hesitation, no equivocation, no variation! My word is your law. Your duty is to obey."

His eyes were like fire, burning across the vast assembly. Millions of fallen angels rose and clapped as their leader left the stage.

3
AFTER EDEN

The next segment showed Lucifer in the same great hall. But the emotional climate there was now much more relaxed. He strode to center stage as his workers rose, applauding. Waving his arms above his head, Lucifer gave a fisted signal of victory. Light glanced off the golden-winged serpent on a chain around his neck. He waited for the applause to die before beginning.

"I greet you in victory. The world is now our kingdom. The man and the woman—the human race—are ours. We have reason to rejoice!" The applause swelled again and the words "Hail, Lucifer, our leader" rang across the assembly.

"We have conquered the human spirit and possessed the human mind," he continued. "Now we shall control them. We will make sure that man chooses against God—and dies.

"Our strategy will focus upon man's everyday cares. Begin by changing into noxious weeds the ferns and flowers man has so affectionately raised. Then infiltrate God's most beautiful plants with poison. As unsuspecting people place them around their dwellings, their children will be attracted by their loveliness and will eat the petals or leaves and be tormented or die. Transform the tiny flying creatures that pollenate the blossoms into insects to be despised by adding a sharp vial of poison to their body. Do not spare man's loyal pets—deform them into vicious creatures of violence and fear. Place in the lions, bears, wolves, and tigers, a ferocity to accompany their great strength.

We must, in short, pervert *everything* God has made."

Applause began anew. The lost angels were in high spirits, drunk with their first victory and their new sense of power. They stamped their feet in time to the clapping until the heavens seemed to vibrate and echo the sound. Lucifer beamed benevolently, caught up in the jubilation. Finally he raised his hands for silence.

"By turning the foods God made into substances that sicken, we will take man's appetite from his control. We will pervert his tastes. By souring his fruits and grains into ingredients of drunkenness, man will be taught to delight in changing the leaves and blossoms of his gardens into substances that lead him into deadly addictions.

"Man must also be taught to pollute his environment, defile his water and poison the very air he breathes until finally his world becomes unlivable. We must help him invent devices—touching everything in his life, from the way he eats to the reason he makes love—to divert him from his Maker. And by tangling the electric currents in his brain to create manias and phobias and all manner of insanities, man can be kept locked away under uncertainty and the fearful prospect of the power of God.

"You are learning well my lessons in deceit. I expect you to follow closely my example in courage, industry and persistence and," he paused dramatically, "in indifference to the threats of God. But I warn you, never be careless. Do not let up on your strategy or attacks for a moment. Each of you must follow the battle plan to the letter. In your assigned post each of you is strictly accountable, through your commander, to me.

"As you well know, our little episode in Eden went according to my plan with one small exception. We are now forced to work under unexpected handicaps, but no matter."

He stopped speaking and looked across the assembly. His under secretary, Raa, caught his eye, questioning. Lucifer gave him an indifferent nod, then went on.

"The Deity has removed the tree of life from the garden. As you know, we had planned on that tree as our insurance for life. Now we are impelled more than ever to thwart any design of the Godhead to return this world to His kingdom. As long as earth is in our control, He is forced to give us life." Lucifer again ignored a gesture by Raa.

"Today I will outline the broad range of my design, concluding with a brief statement on our coming project."

"Be cautious of your claims," Raa motioned. But Lucifer went on.

"Now God the Father has put His plan into effect. He states that the Three devised the plan long before this new world's creation. He is determined to seize this world from my hands. But to do this He must take an impossible risk—the life of His Son. Of course, this may be only a threat. Yet we must take no chances.

"As the recognized ruler of this earth, I am able to meet in the councils of heaven. However, the Father fears me. He no longer confides His plans to me, so we must be prepared for war—days, years, millenniums of war.

"Many of you listened as God explained to Adam and Eve the offerings He requires. He plans for this ritual to carry His message of love and to remind man of the coming sacrifice of the Son. Periodically, Adam will kill a lamb and burn it as a offering before God. God calls it a type of the 'Lamb of God' who is 'to take away the sin of the world.' "

Laughter rippled across the throng. Lucifer nodded, grinning maliciously.

"Oh, those are God's words, not mine. At any rate, we must confound this ridiculous rite and use it to teach man to murder—to kill each other—as well."

His face now changed; a look of uncertainty lingered in his eyes. He leaned on the podium, his large hands curving around its sides.

"I watched that first sacrifice. God instructed Adam, but Adam did the work. They called a lamb, and the foolish creature scampered up to be petted. Then God put a stone in Adam's hand—it seemed to be especially sharpened—and Adam hesitated. You should have seen his pleading expression as he turned to God. If an angel had not strengthened him, he would have fainted. And Eve . . . Eve, did you see her? You would have thought she was watching Adam die!

"But God didn't even speak. Did He dare? He just let Adam tremble and sweat while the lamb lay limp and trusting under his touch. Finally Adam turned his head aside and slit the lamb's throat. Its blood ran down his arm leaving puddles on the ground as the lamb lay limp across his knees." Lucifer's voice fell, then sobered.

"Some of you will recall how Adam looked at God, his face turning pale, and he asked, 'Did I . . . Did I bring this on you?'

"But I don't think many of you heard the next words. God told him something strange, something we must ponder. He said, 'It is well that it hurts. I hope you will always remember that death is the natural result of sin.' "

Lucifer's voice shook. He coughed. "We must not underestimate our opponent."

Nahash, meaning "serpent," fidgeted at Raa's side. Suddenly he stood up. Since he was known for his wisdom, everyone listened closely as he spoke.

"We are impressed by God's dramatics, but couldn't He obliterate us and wipe all memory of us from the minds of His creatures?"

Satan nodded. "It is indeed possible, but His own character does not allow that as long as He holds the absurd idea that He can win by love. The Trinity claims that letting us live and work is the only way to convince the universe that our expulsion is just. But never fear, we will prove His love to be weakness—we will destroy the Son on the very ground that He created."

He leaned forward, his long fingers gesturing.

"Nevertheless, whatever our clever deception of others, we dare not deceive ourselves. If the Godhead should succeed in its so-called 'plan of redemption,' it would prove that liberty comes only from love by granting choice. We must discredit this notion, whatever the cost. Work to confuse liberty with license by advancing freedom without responsibility as the key to happiness. Be prepared to modify our weapons of distraction as necessary from age to age and culture to culture until earth's children are left with no moral character at all.

"When their minds are stripped of values, press in to consume them." Lucifer paused. He had the attention of every listener. He spoke slowly, releasing each word from between clenched teeth: *"We will wipe out the human race."*

As one, the rebellious angels drew in their breath, shocked at the boldness of their leader's plan. Some sat straighter, pride lifting their faces. No matter what the Deity might do to oppose them, with Lucifer, they thought, they would destroy man.

"I repeat, if the Son dares to enter our territory, we have Him in our power. I personally plan to confront Him, to torment Him, to block Him at every turn. By His own laws we *will* destroy Him."

Rasha was visibly agitated. "You warned of overoptimism."

"Can you imagine that the Father would dare perform such an experiment again?" Lucifer replied. His words came faster; his face burned with excitement. "We will have earth's children, we will have the Son. And after that—the universe.

"When God discovers that obedience comes not from love, only from fear, we force Him to give us free access to every corner of His creation." He laughed. "The Father's own sense of justice demands it. But until such time, listen well to these instructions. We must—and you *will*—make every promise of God a lie. We have already succeeded with Adam and his foolish bride. Yet it is possible, even likely, that they will relapse. God's angels still hover near them; He still offers them instruction, and it is obvious that He plans to do more than merely bridge the chasm their choice made between them and heaven. Think," he sneered, "God actually plans friendship with these . . ." Then in afterthought Lucifer swallowed, grimacing as though disgusted, "with these—creatures.

"Keep in mind that we must represent faith in God as something for visionaries, those who have no footing. If any of earth's children persist in their folly of trusting the Father, push them to such wild extremes that their behavior dishonors and discredits that faith rather than upholds God."

Lucifer ignored the unrest developing among his officers.

"You must make surrender to God appear to be an exercise in futility and His instructions a hopeless maze of lies. Lead the most adventuresome of earth's children to make gods of their own creation—an endless parade of gods! The stupid will conform and follow, and soon we'll have them all—the brilliant and the foolish."

He stopped, gathering his thoughts. When Midbar, the one called "Desert," half rose, Lucifer nodded to him. He then stood, gathering his wrap about him.

"I hesitate to speak," he began, "and yet I am confused." He waited, anticipating and receiving a nod from his leader.

"Adam and Eve are still alone. There is no sign of offspring, and yet you speak of untold thousands whom we must lead and confuse and win to our side." Again he stopped, waiting, his pale brow furrowed.

Lucifer eyed him steadily. "You question me, comrade?"

"Oh, no, not at all. I only wonder, will it be as easy as it seems? Will the children of Adam and Eve not be more aware of the"—he hesitated, grasping for the right word—"the *danger* than were their parents?" He sat down, adding, "That is all."

Lucifer smiled benevolently. "An honest question, Midbar, a good question. There shall be offspring in due time. Indeed, the world will be overrun with them. And some will be wary. With these we must use the principle of gradual shock, leading our subjects step by step to our side. Think! Did I overwhelm Eve with theory or did I gradually guide her into distrust of the Three?"

Midbar nodded, remembering.

"Gradually, of course. And so we all will as the years pass. Mark my words, comrades, and remember them. The time is coming when parents shall offer their own children on altars built to me."

A murmur rose from the assembly, but their leader stopped it with his upraised hand.

"You find this hard to believe? Once we get them separated from God, anything we desire from them is a possibility!" He laughed. "Bowing down to images they have made from metal and stone, even worshiping flies and crocodiles is the plan for the years to come."

[Gabriel lowered the sound, his face in agony.

"Watch them laugh," he moaned—"their bodies shaking, feet stomping, mouths wide, and all their fear and hatred of the Godhead smothered by their uproarious laughter. They deemed it funny to picture God's children worshiping a fly." His voice dropped and infinite sadness filled his tone. "And yet before long the children of men did offer their babies to gods of their own making, and then later knelt to worship their gods of perverted imaginations—even flies."

Tears filled his eyes, mirroring my own, but he smiled. "I would not be able to tell you all of this," he reminded himself and me, "if we had not already won the war." Gabriel then continued with the pictures.]

"There will be some," Lucifer went on, "who refuse to bow at our altars. These need not worry us excessively. We plan to merely use a different tactic. We will appear to support God's ministry or priesthood. Those who enjoy this sort of ritual have a special role to play. We will whisper to those who insist on the sacrifice that the Father cannot carry out the task himself so He has to lean on His creatures. By convincing them that they *must* sacrifice or risk God's anger, we will ensnare some. For the rest we will confuse their faith with presumption, making them presume on God's good nature to get them out of all sorts of evil of their own doing.

"In matters relating to God, it is vital for us to excite the emotions of some persons to the exclusion of reason. And yet the converse is also effective for others—letting reason take the place of God. When we perfect this mixture of emotion and reason, we lift their thoughts above God's instructions. God's promises and counsels become apocryphal, a dulled sword, a broken weapon.

"For those creatures who persist in obeying the Father, I have another solution. Simply teach them that God demands they work for His redemption. By keeping them so frantically obeying, they won't have any time for actual worship or friendship with Him. They will see Him as the tyrant I wisely described to you before He expelled us from heaven.

"Our attacks must be engineered to demonstrate that God has turned against His creatures. Remember, my position is to judge you by the cleverness of your counterfeits and by the adroitness of the confusion you create." He smiled broadly, looking over his followers. "You will do it. You *will* do it! Your future in my army is measured by both the quantity and quality of your personal victories. Never forget it!

"In summary," Lucifer said, "our purpose is to simply distract earth's children at every point from becoming acquainted with the Three. Only as they learn to depend upon God will they be able to resist us. It is our business"—his gaze swept the assembly—"it is *your* business to do everything in your power to keep them separated from God. Teach them that their 'God of love' does not really care.

"You must succeed in your tasks," he added. "You know well that I demand no less than perfection." He leaned against the podium. "*Perfection,*" he repeated as if he were greater than God.

"That is all."

The assembly rose, standing in awe while their leader strode away—all except Rasha and Raa who seemed more skeptical than enthusiastic.

"Perfection?" Rasha echoed.

"We shall see," said Raa.

4
PLANS FOR THE FAMILY

When Gabriel presented the next scene, we watched as Lucifer marched to the podium to the accompaniment of a standing ovation and shouts of "Hail, Lucifer." Nodding to the right and left, he raised his hands for silence, then motioned the assembly to be seated. Waiting until the last murmur of adulation faded, he spoke at last.

"Each and every one of you deserves my warmest congratulations on your persistence, and your expertise in leading earth's children to our side. You honor me as your prince by your courage, tenacity, industry and total devotion to our cause. As I am in close touch with your commanders, I am aware of your personal victories." He spoke in character, appealing to their vanity but actually self-serving.

"Today each of you is worthy of the name of Satan, the adversary of God." He gave a little bow, smiling smugly. "You have achieved both the most brilliant and the darkest of works in tearing to shreds Adam's family and in skillfully perverting God's design.

"Now Cain, the first creation of the human race, is in our employ. And Abel"—he raised his hands to still the burst of applause—"Abel, Eve's second offspring and the first human truly to defy us, is dead."

Now Lucifer stood back, relishing the applause, beaming, basking in its expression of praise. Finally, their emotions spent, the self-appointed rulers of earth settled back to listen once again.

"I repeat," Lucifer smiled, "not because you are unaware but for the sheer joy of savoring the words: *Abel is dead.*

"Repeat it," he commanded. "Sing it. Shout it. Let your hearts soar with pride. Already his body lies rotting in the ground, and his parents kneel and weep above it as if their tears could bring him back.

"Remember," he called over the throng. "Remember how Adam hovered over Eve, how he comforted her in her birth pangs. Remember how tenderly they held Cain, their firstborn. Ugly little wrinkled thing, he was, with no hint of the man he would become. But *they loved him.* Ah, that is what breaks their hearts now. *They still love him* . . . and know that their choice in the garden led to his choice against them and against God.

"We have taught them," he laughed, "and I share with you the credit. The knowledge of good *and* evil is a lesson they will never forget, yet is one that their children will repeat a million, yes, a billion times over—and that will just be the beginning.

"And who caused Adam and Eve's grief? Who split Abel's skull, then hurriedly scratched his shallow grave in the ground that received his blood?" Lucifer looked around. "Raa, I must give you much of the credit. You tell us."

Raa, the one named "evil," stood—shoulders tall, head thrown back. "Cain killed him," he called out. "Cain. The firstborn of Adam and Eve. The one they whimsically named 'gift from the Lord.' " Laughter rumbled across the host. "You might say that 'the gift from the Lord' has given himself to us!"

"With Cain's defiance and Abel's defeat, God's plan for animal sacrifices has been dealt a mortal blow." Lucifer began to pace back and forth as he talked.

"We shall make certain that the sacrifice is viewed as a cruel exaction and a requirement of works instead of a symbol of the Son. He calls himself the 'Lamb of God' and planned the sacrifice of a lamb to remind man that He himself will die for them." He stopped short. "Of course that is unlikely. *We* shall conquer earth long before that could occur." He paced faster, his voice thundering. "We will win! We have already won! Adam and Eve's grief is almost more than they can bear. We must *never* let them forget what their 'gift from the Lord' accomplished for us. By continuing to confuse man's faith in God with the sacrifices He requires, man will be unable to understand or fully embrace either.

"We have extraordinary opportunities to create misunderstanding and doubt in the minds of the few who are left. Not that there won't be more children; the earth will be covered with the sons and daughters of Adam. And God plans continued communication with them. He speaks of 'promises' He intends to make with these humans, of rewards when they conform to His law."

[At this point Gabriel stopped the projecter to explain: "Even lecturing his own followers, Lucifer keeps up the pretense that God is not good. Apparently he has actually convinced himself. Lucifer speaks of 'promises and rewards' as though our Father were a merchant bargaining for men's lives. He refuses to acknowledge that men's friendship with God and their dependence upon Him enables God to share His richest blessings. When humans—such as Cain and countless others—turn away, they realize the consequences of separation from God. They hurt."

His voice became gentle. "They are deeply hurt. But the Father hurts even more." Gabriel paused, then restarted the projector.]

"To help the children of earth obey," Lucifer went on, "God offers the aid of His angels, our former comrades who are now aligned against us. As you already know, this sacrifice of lambs is to remind people that the Son himself will die for their sins. God speaks of something He has called 'grace.' It has to do with the Son's perfect life taking the place of their imperfect lives. *As if such a thing were possible!* They do not deserve favor from God, yet they will receive it? Disgusting!"

But Rasha and Raa and even Nabal were not quite so sure that God's greater power would not find a way. Lucifer noticed their questioning glances.

"Do you doubt me?" he asked.

"We are concerned," answered Nabal, "about a possible resurrection."

Lucifer paused, his face a puzzle. This was his staff chief explaining that all was not clear how God planned to give Abel life. "We are now independent, separated from God. Yet we do not die. Perhaps, perhaps the Father merely threatens."

Lucifer straightened. His manner changed. "Ebed," he said. "Your ideas are good. Tell your comrades of what we spoke in our pre-session."

Ebed rose, his face shining with the pride of a slave singled out for praise by his master. "We plan to lead earth's children to presume upon God for His blessings without being fully committed to His plan. This presumption"—Ebed stopped, looking around, enjoying the role of teacher—"this presumption—expecting God's care and rewards without obeying His commands—will bring them lives of despair."

Lucifer smiled his thanks and, with a nod, motioned his servant to be seated. "Ariun," he called to another commander, "is Cain happy now?"

Low laughter spread across the assembly. They knew the answer but Ariun, the "cunning one," spoke for them. "He is in the depths of despair. By his own choice he is separated from his family and from the Trinity. And yet," Ariun smiled, "he does not accept our solace."

Lucifer nodded. "Time will change things; his ranks will increase, but now he is driven and alone." He smiled. "Others will follow. The babies that will delight Adam and Eve and stem their grief will mature and turn from God. It will be easy to lead them to confuse presumption with the obedience of faith. We will so confound them that in desperation they will turn to other gods, worshiping anything, everything: peoples and animals, stars and trees, and organs of their bodies. In short, they will worship us instead of God, for we are, in fact, their choice when they presume upon Him."

He leaned forward, his eyes boring into the assembled throng, pausing for emphasis. "I direct you to use every imaginable device to cause the child's actions, like those of Cain, to so perplex his parents that they despair the day he was conceived and damn the Creator for giving them the ability to have young. As the child emerges toward adulthood, excite in him all manner of selfishness and morbid curiosity. Sow thoroughly the seeds of rebellion, distrust, disloyalty and hate, that our way may thrive in the name of their self-worth which it counterfeits and destroys." Lucifer saw that he was making his point well.

"Never mind if your work of destruction and death appears to reflect on me. Distract from God in every way you can. Make earth's children think they are deceiving us when in fact we know them better than they know themselves. This will be a continual challenge, for you must deviously mix the themes of God with subtle barbs and lewd temptations. For instance, confuse love with lust and self-serving goals."

The demons applauded. Even Rasha and Raa were impressed.

Lucifer held up his hand. "Don't forget the lessons we learned from our victory over Abel. We cannot afford the challenge of many like him. We must so distract man and woman from God that they blame Him for their problems and turn away even more from His conditions. As they separate themselves from Him, He will be forced to remove His cover further from them. Soon they and their children and even their flocks will be naked before us."

"They already are," Raa interrupted.

"Of course, Evil One," he retorted. "But I speak more deeply than you understand. They will be naked not only of garments but of all defense before our work as accusers of 'the brethren.' "

Raa nodded, satisfied, and Lucifer continued.

"When they build, you will tear down; when they restore, burn them out; when they repent, remark on the futility of confession and demand that they must plead and plead and plead again for forgiveness—as if their God cannot hear them. So fill them with guilt that they cannot believe that He forgives. When they succeed in any venture, unless that success supports our cause, plague them with the uncertainty that it is too good to be true. And even then your wisdom may dictate a more skillful attack: discouragement, depression or despair. But in using these, among the most effective of your tools, take care that you yourselves do not become entrapped. Discouragement is only for man. It means for him a weakness of his faith in God. His despondency will then fracture and eventually shatter that faith.

"On the other hand, tempt people to be self-satisfied, utterly independent of God, until tragedy strikes. Then watch them fall apart. Look at what Abel's death has done to Adam and Eve. At such moments oppress them with anguish. It will be easier at such times for them to turn to us instead of to God. As they come to us for their answers, be ready to accommodate their every wish.

"It is essential now, even more than before, that the children of earth rely more on emotions than reason. And when reason is their tool, it must be used without the direction of the Creator. See that the Holy Spirit, which would remind them of God's love and plan, is turned away at every point so that as they ponder, only our messages will be clear. Their feelings must be their guides."

He leaned on the podium. "The theme for today's lecture has been 'conquering the human family.' I am almost through. Yet there remains one important point.

"In the gift of procreation we find outstanding opportunities to make demons of men. You will find that we can debase every good gift of God to man. Sex is no exception. Notice God's design for this gift—as an extension of His own creative power. He planned that it should be a unique bond between a man and a woman, a sharing of themselves with each other under the blessing of God. It is an emotion and a principle that reflects the intimate bond between the Godhead themselves.

"But never mind. We will twist God's purpose until His creative gift supports our cause. By making every effort to deprive the human sexual encounter of the mystery and winsomeness which the Creator designed, another of God's tools becomes ours.

"Cause man and woman to use the act for their own selfishness, unmindful of the needs of their partners. Strip away the spiritual and emotional sides of their relationships, and make them build on the physical alone. Teach them that sex is their right, that it carries no responsibility—if it feels good, do it with whomever they choose."

He laughed raucously. "This will serve a dual purpose. Sexual encounters of this nature will tear down their self-worth as children of God. It separates them emotionally and spiritually, even while they, for the moment, are together in body. And then, observing this abuse, many of God's other children can be convinced—in ignorance and self-righteousness—that sex is so destructive that it comes from me. Many will be driven from sex as an expression of love to the other extreme. Marriages, even those which claim to thrive on God's love, will be destroyed.

"Further ravaging of this intimate union can be accomplished by leading man to take to himself more than one wife. We will first arrange for him to find a second woman. Then, as generations move on, it becomes natural for him to share his attentions with many. Of course, it is impossible to give yourself totally to more than one person, so we will stir animosities which will survive the centuries. Bear in mind that marriage is a symbol of God's undivided devotion to the unity of His family. We will sever man from God.

"When we disrupt marriage, when we make the dissolution of marriage vows of no consequence, when we divide parents, we will destroy their offspring who, in logical sequence, will be deprived of self-value. They shall hate their parents and turn away from God. To many, marriage will come to possess no security. They will change partners with little more thought than they give to changing their clothes.

"We will destroy the family!"

5
THE THREAT OF ENOCH

As the next picture flashed on the great screen we saw Lucifer's most important team members assembled in his inner sanctum. Nabal, the chief of staff, Skahor, Hoshek, Moot—to name only a few of his commanders—all awaited their prince who would enter only after all the others had arrived.

There had been whispers that this was more than a routine planning and briefing session. Lucifer had returned from the Universe Council meeting with a new look in his eyes. Was it elation? Puzzlement? No one could guess. God didn't tell him everything, they realized. Often they wondered if their leader received much information at all from the heavenly council. Of course, as self-proclaimed leader of earth, he demanded and received the right to attend.

Speculation vibrated against the richly polished walls of Lucifer's private room where he rarely invited anyone. Had they been called in for censure? His anger could be terrifying. Herev, "the sword," spoke up loudly as if to rehearse for a ploy for Lucifer's favor, asserting that earth had never been in better condition nor had earth's creatures ever been more under their control.

"But what about Enoch?" Moot wryly suggested, quickly discerning Herev's possible ploy.

The very air seemed to crackle with hostility at the mention of Enoch's name. "What about—?" someone started to argue, as the door swung open and Lucifer strode in.

They stood instantly, conversation stopped in mid-word. All eyes were upon him. They could not help but feel pride in his appearance and the nobility of his bearing.

He grinned and motioned them to be seated. They complied, relaxing, basking in his smile.

"I greet you," he said.

"In the name of pride in our triumph, and the deceiving of our enemy's creation, you have lived up to my expectations. You have literally destroyed the human family. Under your influence, flaunting the statutes of God has become a rule of their lives." Lucifer paused dramatically, weighing each word for its full impact. "God has become angry indeed. Earth's children—*our* children—find the prescriptions He has given for human happiness to be void of wisdom. They disregard His every word, and we now have Him on the defensive. God has determined to shorten man's life because of his insatiable drive to follow us. Can't you see how God is playing into our hands? We will use this decision to confound His design further."

He stopped, letting the applause swell until it echoed and reverberated beyond their walls. When it had died to a spatter of sound, he spoke again.

"I have summoned you, my select leaders, because of a new development. This unique happening may bring final victory to us. I will not talk long with you today, for every moment is a precious stone in our crown of defiance. We must never relax our vigilance lest God's angels gain entrance into the minds we hold captive. You have been exceptionally effective in making man an embarrassment to his Creator, so much so that he has exhausted the divine patience. Man has murdered, plundered and lived a lie. He has profaned the name of the God of heaven and desecrated the memory of His followers by incestuous and brutish behavior. For many years he has bowed to gods of our creation, to images he has formed by his own hand. And he takes to himself and his gods all the glory which we know is due only to the Creator. Yet we have no caution to spare."

He was pacing now, lecturing himself as much as his followers.

"When a person does turn to God, and some will, despite our efforts, you must punish him again and again for his sins. Make him believe that guilt and punishment are heaven's expected reward. Ply him with self-condemnation. Tempt him to believe that victory over sin is impossible, that God is cruelly unforgiving.

"If he insists on worshiping the Creator, devise ways of turning worship and introspection and meditation unto God into an exercise of self-satisfaction and an accusation of those who don't. Use any and every stratagem to turn man's mind away from God.

"When he still persists in worship, taunt him in his prayers. Suggest to him that he call and call and call on the name of God. Make it seem as though only repetition of God's name will awaken the Deity to humanity's cries. Fill his prayers with meaningless repetitions which crowd out sacred thought. As he shouts, 'Lord! Lord! Lord!' make forgiveness seem further and further away. In his futility he will turn to us for his only comfort—which we will supply in our most malevolent way."

"But not all will do this," reminded Moot. "How about Enoch?"

"You are right; the man Enoch personally caused me great alarm and has threatened our kingdom. Though almost all of his generation have followed our leading, he has remained pure. We have raped mankind, plundering their very souls, and the beauty of it is that the stupid creatures think they are following their own inventions." His smile faded. "Enoch is a puzzlement, however. Everyone around Enoch, from great-grandparents to the children playing at their feet, has danced to our music. Yet Enoch seemed tuned only to the music of heaven. And because of his 'perfection' amidst our pollution, God took him to heaven without allowing him to taste death."

"But not all around Enoch have yet danced to us," spoke Moot again.

Lucifer was annoyed, but his nod conceded Moot's point.

He shuddered visibly. "God tricked us, taking Enoch out of our control. I made that clear to Him at the Council, but—you know 'the Father,' " he added sarcastically. "He would not argue with me.

"Now Enoch's son Methuselah appears daily closer to his father's course. We cannot afford any more Enochs. They distort our blueprint and open up avenues for the Godhead that we must keep closed. It is imperative that we reevaluate our stratagems. That is why I have called you, my highest commanders, to this emergency meeting. You must shortly report my decisions in your regional conferences.

"I direct your attention and your most creative efforts to the man Noah. He pleases the Deity altogether too much. And his family has dared to obstruct our most insidious efforts to fracture their loyalties to each other and to God. Yet we need them as our agents. We must somehow break the resistance of Noah's family. No matter how long they spurn our way, we cannot surrender them to God. There is no greater weapon in our arsenal than the ungodly family. The marriage vow has lost most of its significance. Men and women discard partners as children discard toys."

There was a rush of applause and a murmur of approval.

"He expects to save man and beast in a most elementary and comical way: God has chosen Noah to build a great boat! They will call it an ark, and God plans to save all who follow Noah into it. As Noah builds, he is to call man to repentance . . . and salvation. The notion, of course, is absurd. People will never be disturbed by fear of water. With the ground watered from subterranean channels and by dew, they have never seen rain. We will use their ignorance to destroy any lingering faith in God and to heap ridicule upon Noah and his Savior." He jeered, "Imagine a ship without water to float it!"

His forefinger tapped his desk. "Not only do I direct you to plague the people with doubts and the vilest possible innuendo about Noah's prophecies of the coming flood, but bewilder Noah and his family and any helpers at every step. Confuse their understanding of God's design for the boat. Throw their plans into disarray. Create havoc with their materials. Disarrange and disfigure the joints of their wood. Dull their tools. Make it impossible for them to work in a satisfying way so that they are abashed in their folly. Make them a laughing stock before their neighbors and any who come to view their fiasco."

"What kind of a ship is this to be?" asked Nabal. "It would have to be a monster to do all you describe!"

"The ship," Lucifer answered, "is planned to be about 150 meters long, about 17 meters wide and about 10 meters high. Large as that may be, any child can see of course that it will hold only a few persons and animals. That is what makes the whole notion so ridiculous."

"Where," again interrupted Skahor, "will they build this thing?"

"Probably on a mountianside," Lucifer replied, "and we will make the most of the spectacle of a big boat being built high on dry land with no sizeable body of water in sight."

The assembled group laughed with Lucifer and Skahor.

"Furthermore, by the Creator's own design, it takes male and female to reproduce. So He will have to save at least two of each animal kind." Lucifer laughed again, shaking his head. "Noah will never have room for those beasts, and if somehow he manages, we will so confuse and stampede the animals that he will never get them into the boat."

The demons looked around at each other, relishing the prospect of embarrassing Noah and God.

"We now have God on the run," railed Nabal.

"We will force Him into evermore impossible situations and futile acts," echoed Moot.

"Yet," Lucifer warned, as he fixed his commanders with a stern look, "the pride and arrogance with which we infuse men and contrive their fall must never be allowed to consume us. Our mission is to deceive man; we dare not deceive ourselves. It is imperative that we outmaneuver the agents of God, but you will not be forgiven if you are entrapped yourselves. Remember, we can afford no more Enochs. Your orders are to make Noah and his sons like we are—adversaries of God."

Then speaking in a low and slow voice, he concluded, "I am sure you have now found that there is no wisdom in a physical attack against the angels of God or against any man who has placed his life under God's control. The physical power of our former comrades is clearly beyond us. In most cases our assaults must be more peripheral than frontal, more mental than physical. We must deceive man before we can destroy. We will work to make him trust in himself more than in God—as did Eve. Thus, in relying on himself, he will actually be following us. This tactic is the key to our certain success."

The high officers stood and bowed as Lucifer rose to leave, with Nabal at his side.

6
FRUSTRATIONS OF A FLOOD

As the picture hit the screen, we watched Lucifer walk slowly, shoulders hunched, hands behind his back. His commanders—those closest to him and his dream—followed. Mile after mile they plodded across the raw, ravaged ground.

Mud sucked at Lucifer's feet, and now and then he stopped to scrape them against a jagged rock. Head down, it seemed he could not bear to look across the vast expanse at the cataclysm, but kept his gaze on the few square yards before him.

By now, months after the Deluge, the water had drained to cover a mere three-fourths of the earth's surface. Ragged mountains loomed where deer had raced across emerald plains. Oceans covered man's elaborate gardens for his gods.

Immense conglomerates of forests and animal bones, tossed together and covered with dirt and rocks, were silhouetted against the horizon. Lucifer looked ahead, then averted his gaze. Now and then he muttered something, but when his followers jerked forward to listen, he had nothing to reply.

Silently they skirted a vast plain crisscrossed with stilled rivers of lava. Far in the distance a cone-shaped mountain thrust up its purple head.

Above, a small brown finch circled and sang. It seemed alien in that barren land.

The sun had climbed to its zenith, then begun to slide toward the naked hills. Gonev whispered to his comrade. "Odd thing, the sun. With all our power we can't throw a line across it and halt its march across the sky."

Rasha shrugged. "Perhaps our leader has less power than he thought," he answered cautiously.

The solemn group walked on. Now and again Lucifer motioned toward a chasm or a half-buried pyramid of bleaching bones. His comrades wondered how long his reverie would last. When he asked them to walk with him, they sensed he planned to break his silence that had begun with the Deluge. But the day wore on with Lucifer speaking only in the same brooding monosyllables of the past months.

He stopped abruptly on a plateau covered with water-rounded boulders and nodded to indicate they should sit down.

"We will not linger here," he began. "But I have a few things of extreme importance to tell you." His voice sounded hollow. His followers exchanged looks that he did not see.

"We are baffled by the strange antics of God," he continued. "Clearly we underestimate Him. We must redouble our efforts to anticipate every possible turn He might take to defeat us." He looked across his comrades. "We continue to hold a crucial advantage: In order to take the world back from us, the Father must sacrifice His Son. Such an attempt to rescue this little group of human beings risks His eternal loss. I don't believe the Father is either so prodigal in His methods nor so generous with His creatures as to take such a chance. Nevertheless, we are left with no room for error."

The demon lieutenants glanced furtively around to note their comrades' reactions to Lucifer's conjectures. They realized that doubt had also flooded their master's previously confident mien. And they had some questions on his mental consistency.

"Obviously the threatened flood did overflow the earth," he observed. "Anyone with clear vision can see that the depths of the earth were broken up. God freed fountains that we didn't know existed, and the power of water . . ." His voice trailed off, then momentarily brightened. "Of no matter. We will make use of that power later." Then he lapsed again into deep thought.

In many places they could see that earthquakes caused the layers of the earth to literally stand on edge; vast forests of giant trees were buried deep in the earth. They shook their heads as if to dislodge the memory.

"We failed," observed Gonev, "to see that the Creator could direct the animals to seek voluntary entrance to the ark without the frustration of a comical roundup by Noah."

Anger flashed in Lucifer's eyes. His voice was coarse as he declared, "We underestimate God."

"Who is doing this underestimating?" inquired Raa facetiously.

"We shall no longer be flushed with our success," said Lucifer, ignoring Raa. "In actual fact, our success in debasing the human race was more widespread than even we knew. By the time we had done our work and the Creator had retrieved His few faithful by laying them aside in death—for His mythical resurrection and reward—only Noah's family remained." He smiled. "A victory, a triumph over God, to be sure. But in the future we will not underestimate Him.

"It is time for us to carry out our plan for the earth's only human survivors—Noah, his wife, his three sons, and their wives. I am appointing certain of you to bedevil each person every moment of the day and into every night. I expect you to distract them from God, to corrupt them, to defile them, and to tempt them to hoard the few things they were able to save for themselves. Inflict them with selfishness, for that will divide them. Make them long for what they lost. Overwhelm them with discouragement and despair. We will never have another time when our large forces can concentrate on so few." The falling sun cast long shadows across the clot of evil angels. Their leader began to pace.

"Moot and Hoshek, command your servants to stir up the cruelest instincts of the beasts so that they will disrupt the lives of earth's children. Lead them to attack man from fear, even to kill.

"You will turn the gardens of Noah's family into graves of disappointment by warping his vineyards and his groves. Give him trees with few roots, leaves without fruit. Fill his grain baskets with briars; plague his feet with thistles until he cries out against God and seeks solace from us.

"In the times ahead we are committed to obliterating from the minds of men their recollections of the works of God." He smiled at his followers. "Your brilliant manipulation of Eve set a high standard for your future. See that Noah's grandchildren consider the flood no more than their fathers' bad dream. Eventually we will relegate it to mythology, that men may forget the lessons of divine judgment as they have forgotten Eden's devastation. Finally, we shall plant in their minds concepts of evolution to inure them against the idea of a personal Creator and God." These were exciting words to the demons.

"Never mind that man will be unable to plumb the ultimate sources of life. Keep him so busy with conjecture—the fruit of his own reason—that he takes lightly God's words. Keep him so hostile and disbelieving of the story of God's creation that even in professing to know and trust God he will, in fact, deny Him. Cain was a model of our genius, you know."

"Just how do we go about this?" challenged Hoshek.

"Throughout the ages, those who suggest creation's possible truth we will accuse of paranoia and flights of the imagination. By bringing scorn against those who warn of man's future destruction, we can successfully make them objects of ridicule by men both of science and philosophy." Lucifer now warmed to Hoshek's question. His voice rang in the gathering twilight.

"Persuade men to take their future into their own hands. I plan a tower for them to build into the clouds. There they will seek wisdom from the stars and try to shape their own destiny. Keeping them so busy with their self-aggrandizement, they will have no time to sustain a relationship of trust in their God."

The great one lapsed into a moment's reverie at this thought.

The moon rose slowly, a golden disc, its light falling in pale pools across the clustered group. Moot raised his hand, then spoke at his leader's nod.

"I'm excited about the possibility of working with food," he said. "Remember our delight in playing with the genes and chromosomes of the plants—"

"Thorns on roses," Lucifer agreed. "Poison in petals." Then he looked at Moot. "You have a question?"

"Surely for many we can go beyond food," Moot said. "We

have already used a variety of wines and other intoxicants to control the minds and emotions of many who would otherwise resist our seductions."

Lucifer nodded. "Your mind works with mine, Moot," he smiled. "Shortly I will be using several of our legions in a project to defile Noah. Alcohol is our only method short of death to deprive this otherwise impregnable character of sound judgment. We will manage his defeat without his even knowing that he is dealing with us.

"Once we have made Noah repugnant to his family and his family to him, we will extend the dissension to his descendants until we create total confusion. We will then raise up a king among men and make him a counterfeit of God. Throughout the years we can develop many counterfeits, my surrogates who will forge a chain of wars in the name of righteousness but who will actually rape the family of God until a generation emerges that shall make the antedeluvians look like saints.

"And man's curiosity is immense," grinned Raa.

"Yes," agreed the leader. "He is eager to understand everything beyond the limits of his mind. Here is another tool to degrade him, ultimately insuring his collapse. We must constantly feed this fetish to know beyond the knowable—in appetite, in sex, in every triviality, but especially when it concerns the nature of God. Though humans and angels alike can never fully comprehend the Deity, we will drive man to doubt. As they seek answers that are beyond their understanding, we can goad them into impatience, imprudence and atheism.

"Even more, we must make certain that man believes the Deity is not Three in One but three distinct and separate Gods—if gods at all. Lead men to conjecture that if three, then why not more? As I told you before, we shall give man all the gods he demands. For those who love inventing new gods, fill their cup with delight. For those who still want one God alone, promote its perversion to the maximum as long as it plays them into our hands."

Lucifer stepped upon a low rock, waiting as the applause swelled, then died.

"Drive man to expediency," he commanded. "See that his

faith cringes in the face of obeying God's commands. Turn faith into presumption; see that man demands blessings without obedience. When they do obey, see that it is from fear more than from love. When faith is so blinded, make the presumptuous seem like men of vision. Make God look like me, your master devil, and man will come to me as they once came to God.

"We will invent a myriad of devices to stupefy man in his search for God. Give them the spiritualistic game and a ball of mystery to further tantalize their curiosity. You commanders must carefully orient your servants in the use of this crystal ball. Thousands of our agents will peer into them and obtain messages from us thinking they came straight from heaven. Gullible man will thrive on our deceit."

A sudden wind whipped Lucifer's clothes. He called out to be heard above it.

"Some of you may wonder at my schemes; some question how I dare to plan for millions when a mere eight survived the flood. We must not limit ourselves because of God's small victory. When it became apparent that all earth's children would die in the tidal waves and the earthquakes that accompanied the rain, I was puzzled as to what our next step should be. But now I am convinced that we must plan for the millions yet unborn. We cannot waste a precious minute in regret that God saved the eight. We simply begin our attack anew."

A hush covered the group as the moon slid behind a cloud and they sat in darkness. Then latent applause began for their leader, and he called over their clapping.

"Our reward will be the eternal death of earth's children, their separation from God forever. What else have we to give them? I charge you to give of your best!"

The applause grew, swelled with their laughter and echoed across the darkened vale.

7
THE GENERATION OF THE UNASHAMED

We watched the next segment of the panorama with great interest as, walking proud and tall, Lucifer climbed the steps to the platform. Behind him light poured through colored glass, framing him with a rainbow glow. He scanned his assembled followers, his eyes darting to the farthest rim of the standing, applauding demon angels. Face beaming, eyes glinting, he motioned for his servants to be seated.

"It is with particular appreciation today that I hail your achievements of recent centuries. I am well-informed by your commanders on the regional conferences they have held with you. First today, our plan to corrupt the family of Noah was successful."

Applause resounded through the great hall. Lucifer smiled, then raised his hand.

"Noah, as I'm sure you recall, planted a vineyard, harvested the grapes and, as God's own sun warmed them, with a little help from us they fermented into wine." Laughter bubbled among the multitude. "Ah, Noah, thirsty—and ignorant—drank and drank until he passed out on the floor of his tent.

"His drunkenness in turn brought defilement from his own son which gave us the opening to bewilder and corrupt his descendants. In due time we caused separation in his family that endures to this day, dividing father and son, brother against brother. Such a scene is my delight!

"You, my comrades, have done well. Hoshek and Queren, I particularly commend your leadership today. We have made family rise against family and nation against nation. Rasha, you were brilliant in the Babel project. We were not deterred," he shrugged, "by the Creator's confounding their language to prevent completion of the Babel Tower. So the world is no longer of one tongue. We will show him how to change speech. He has handed us a tool of confusion that we will use to embarrass Him forever.

"Be sure you know the languages well, and memorize the mores and the folkways as new tribes and nations develop. These are destined to be crucial tools of deceit as our conflict continues with a desperate God. We intend to set races against each other by pitting the children of Ham against the children of Shem and drawing a color line. The possibilities are endless. Our plans include the creation of minorities and castes and then convincing the stronger and wealthier to abuse them. They will remain a cord of perplexity to man which we will weave throughout the fabric of societies as long as men live and die on the earth."

Referring to man's shorter life after the flood, Lucifer continued, "It will force him to rely on written records to replace the oral testaments handed down by the long-lived antedeluvians. But this gives us an opportunity to forge and counterfeit and confuse these records until they can be interpreted to present *our* goals to man. With them, we can convince earth's creatures that we hold the key to their most exciting and satisfying future." His smile grew hideous. "Never mind that they elect death over life.

"Yet it would be folly today if we did not acknowledge an impediment to our goals. Can you guess, Raa? You have been his guardian."

Raa stood, anger fighting with embarrassment in his face. "His name is Abram," he said. "I have tried—"

Lucifer broke in. "I do not censure you, friend. I know you and your comrades have tried. I, too—" his voice unraveled, then grew brisk. "Unless we destroy Abram's usefulness, it is possible that he will be used to destroy us. You may not be aware that God has reached into Chaldea, the southern setting of our own Babylon, a citadel of our strength, to call this character to form a new nation. God refers to it as a "chosen nation" and promises untold blessings to Abram and his children if they continue to trust and follow Him.

"I will not defer to this crass challenge! This man can be tricked and controlled as we did with Adam, again working through a woman—Abram's beautiful wife.

"We intend to drive Abram out of Canaan, the land God has chosen for him. He will not dare to return to Haran, his homeland, for fear of offending God. To the east is desert and to the west lies only the Mediterranean Sea. So our man will be trapped. Gerar and Gaza and Egypt are lands of plenty and provide the perfect setting to entice him there. He has a large extended family with servants and beasts galore. They must eat. Abram's faith in God's ability to provide is lacking and can be used to force him into our grasp. The moment his entourage arrives, Raa, who heads this operation, is to see that word is passed to the king. The ruler, who is always looking for beautiful women, will take Sara to his harem as a price for the lives of Abram and his camp. Can you imagine what that will do to him? His trust in God will be shattered.

"When the patriarch returns to Canaan, we must meet him with more trouble. Stir up his relatives in family quarrels for shares of the divine blessing. His nephew Lot is particularly weak. And Lot's wife is selfish and demanding. Use her—through him—to divide the fledgling nation. By inducing Lot to accuse Abram of greed, we can then entice Lot to the valley that some of you have been preparing. Rasha, this is your specialty," he said, smiling benevolently. "Tell us the names of your special projects."

Rasha, the "wicked one," rose and bowed. "I call them Sodom and Gomorrah," he replied. "I and my comrades will make those cities so evil that their very names will become a symbol of wickedness for all time."

Lucifer thanked him with a nod.

"Are you curious," Rasha grinned, "about the tactic we intend to employ?"

"Tell us," replied Lucifer, a bit superciliously.

Rasha was not ruffled. "We will pervert man to lie with man and tempt women to prefer sex with women. This grand plot further distorts God's plan of natural love and procreation. It was *your* idea."

Lucifer was obviously delighted. "Continue," he urged.

"We have committed ourselves," added Rasha, "to make it the generation of the unashamed."

"Poetic," mused Lucifer. " 'The generation of the unashamed.' It will be a model for all time of reckless wastefulness and lust, of self-serving license, amusement and vice."

Rasha nodded, basking in the repulsive smile of his master.

"See that you bring Lot's wife into their revelries, and her children with her," Lucifer admonished. "Go easy on her at first. Lead her away from God in easy steps. Sodom must have more to offer them then lewdness and sex. Parties, good foods, fine wine and flattering friends. As the Lots succumb, they must be immersed in the social life of the city. Lot, too, must be made fearful of crossing his wife—a disruptive example to be used from generation to generation to destroy godly homes.

"But we won't forget Abram," he added. "We will take every measure to destroy his greatest strength, his trust in God, working through his family and those closest to him. We must keep him uncertain about their loyalty to him and disrupt the Deity's plans for multiplying him into a nation, creating embarrassment for God and for Abram's lines for all time." He struck the podium with his fist. "We must not—we will not!—allow this newly chosen nation to survive as a channel of divine blessings.

"And Ariun." Lucifer turned to the cunning one.

"Yes?" Ariun answered cautiously.

"You must sharpen your tools of pride and greed, and your comrades must continue to study and refine your techniques of placing portraits of truth in frames of error. God specifies that Abram and his new nation completely surrender to His 'loving' ways." Lucifer snickered and laughter rocked the assembly at the word "loving."

"You are to make sure that man obeys not from faith and

love for God but as a fearful response to the arbitrary and self-serving demands of a divine dictator."

Suddenly his face froze into a mask of hatred as he spat curses against the Father. "We are stronger!" he cried. "We will seed their minds with presumption so they will make demands of God without full obedience in return, confuse love with every kind of indulgence, and dilute God's truth with selected morsels of deceit."

"Yes," agreed Ariun, "our legions are committed to lose no opportunities to cast slurs upon the Deity and to denounce the angels as Their vindictive agents. We will imply that angels are actually weak and afraid of the Father."

"Exactly," exulted Lucifer. "Don't ever let Abram's family forget the folly of the Deity's historic plan. See that his nation chooses our wisdom over God's."

Now he leaned over the podium, his large hands as usual clutching it.

"Now I must repeat certain general aspects of our attack. Do you hear me, Nabal?" Lucifer looked sharply at his key officer, who seemed momentarily distracted.

"Why, yes; yes, sir," was the prompt reply.

"This is the most sober of warnings. We must make no mistakes. There is no room for any of you to be clumsy or brash. Take nothing for granted. We must destroy this new nation. Remember our goal: to so depress, discourage and produce despair that man eventually forgets God as 'the Great Giver.'"

The demons cheered hysterically.

"When man turns from God," he smiled, his voice lowering to a dramatic whisper, "he must turn to us."

The response was a wild and cheering ovation.

"Be kind to earth's foolish children when kindness is required to deceive. Be gentle when appropriate, to divert prejudice against us. Be affectionate when necessary, to draw man to you. Bless him when blessings will dispel his caution, reward him with prosperity when it turns him from God. Keep his mind on himself, dilute his self-control, and, when it serves our purposes, shower him with all his wants. Satisfy all his curiosities. It's easy enough to meet all his demands if that will distract him from God and weaken—eventually shatter—his will to serve Him.

"As I did with Eve, we will do with all," he directed. "Color the commands of God. Laugh with earth's children, cry with them, ruffle them, soothe them, do anything to keep them from knowing sin by its right name. Let us fulfill in our own way God's promise to make Abram's new nation indeed like the sands of the sea—awash with doubts and defiance. And his descendants like the stars—the stars that fell from heaven!"

The meeting broke up with laughter and standing applause. As the panorama faded, Gabriel looked at me solemnly. "Remember," he said, "Lucifer's ultimate goal for you and all men—is death."

8
THE DIVIDING OF A NATION

Lucifer's now typical preamble again came on the screen. "Greetings in the name of blasphemy and defiance," he grinned from his dais above his assembled angel followers; "for we freely blaspheme and spit in the eyes of the God of heaven. We are succeeding in the disruption of the divine plan for earth's children. Our latest victory, I predict, will become the anathema of anathemas—the curse of curses—to both man and God through the ages." He stopped, waiting for the applause to ebb. "I speak, of course, of our division of Abraham's family.

"We have destroyed the family of Lot. When angels came to rescue them before the destruction of Sodom, they were reluctant, as you know, to leave. So his wife died in disobedience. His only two remaining daughters used wine, our old friend, to drug Lot into such a stupor that they could make him the father of their sons." Lucifer's laughter seemed to gurgle from some hellish fountain deep within him, and all the demons laughed with him.

"Oh, I have great plans for those boys. They are to become the heads of nations that we will use to attack God's 'chosen nation.'

"Abraham himself has lost faith in his family—God's chosen people—and for good reason. I commend you, comrades. Many of God's community have welcomed the vilest of behavior.

"But far more important, as you will eventually see, we have turned the Deity's test of Abraham's faith into a wholesale disruption of God's design. How can this chosen nation now carry God's message to the world? Who is going to trust these people?"

"But," interrupted Rasha, "God has used some surprising techniques."

Lucifer flashed an angry glance at the demon and went on.

"We succeeded in using Sarah to question God's promise of a son. At her insistence—and by our blueprint—Abraham took the maid Hagar to his bed. Oh, they are so easily led. That not only violated God's principle of one wife for one man but has also created a dilemma which will haunt the patriarch and his descendants for all time."

He laughed, flushed with the recollection of his success.

"I plan to personally see that project through. I guarantee that the descendants of Abraham's firstborn, Hagar's son Ishmael, will clash with the descendants of Sarah's son Isaac. One day you will more fully appreciate the chaos this family feud can create."

His mood changed. He paced the platform, his head down.

"But before we detail these plans, I have a solemn admonition and rare admission of failure. We were stupid in our manipulation of Abraham and the powerful king of Gerar. We took King Abimelech for granted. We assumed correctly that he would be so taken with Sarah's beauty that he would demand her for his harem or even as his queen. Our work was carefully executed on Abraham. We relied correctly on his willingness to lie that she was his sister, sacrificing her for their safety in the land. But we vaguely assumed God would be indifferent, and we were careless in our attention to the king. When he actually discovered that she was Abraham's wife, he gave her up without even laying a warm hand on her.

"We should have moved closer to him years before. Why didn't we anticipate the dreams and warnings God can use to frighten even a king? He was loath to violate those cautions in spite of his desire to enlarge his harem with a beautiful woman and the 'sister' of an important man. It is imperative that in the future we turn human minds to such self-serving pride and licentiousness that they will be hardened to visions from God. We must destroy man's heart! Do you understand?" Lucifer looked out over the demonic crowd, his every glance a challenge.

Some nodded. Many said, "Yea, yea."

"We must destroy man's conscience," he continued, "no matter how loyal he may seem to God! Righteousness is to us a deadly potion; let us dilute it with sin."

"But," demurred Raa, "we are having some trouble with visitors from above."

Lucifer was quick to answer. "We cannot prevent the clever visits of heaven's angels to persons such as Abraham, but I shall hold you accountable for dulling man's sense of right and wrong so as to thwart every angel's mission. If we can make people indifferent to heavenly values—integrity, initiative, industry, responsibility and morality—we reduce their productivity and self-respect. The loss of these qualities ruins both a man and a nation. When we destroy man's value system, the finer graces God is trying to develop are sacrificed. I speak of patience and compassion, of course. Disgusting qualities. Then there are forbearance, forgiveness, meekness, trust, and love for their neighbors.

"Without these, the person is our slave. His faith in God is dead and, thus separated from God, he too must die. God requires an open, trusting relationship with these creatures," he added. "When they no longer trust Him, they are ours. It's easy enough then to possess them.

"We were also incautious with Lot. We relied almost wholly upon using his wife to deceive him, and this was an error that we dare not repeat!" His fist slammed again on the podium. "Hear me well! With God, even a weak Lot can be a strong adversary for us. We must never again make the mistake of working through a woman while ignoring the man. It is simple enough to divert humans from God. Cram their days with triviality. Puzzle them with incidentals. Tailor a few vices to their personal tastes. And make them become so self-centered that they are hardened to anyone else's needs. It matters not with what you fill their minds, just so they are too busy for anything more than a superficial relationship with God.

"Enough of that," he said. "Let's turn our attention to the harassment of Abraham and his children. Hagar and Ishmael's exile is only the preface to my plan. Not only can we extend the cleavage between Hagar's and Sarah's sons, but we can tear apart Isaac's family and their offspring. We will make them a regret to God. In every generation let us take care to disrupt the family of the son God chooses to bless, for his progeny will be the royal line of God's people. Harass that nation until its people turn on the God who chose them. Separated from God, they will lose their value as His witnesses, and one day they will no longer be His chosen race. The promised Messiah must become anathema to God's people, and they anathema to God."

"Just how," challenged Nabal, "do you suggest we do this?"

Lucifer first looked fiercely at him, then seemed to relent as an indulgent master.

"Remember without fail, my fellow liar, that the key to the success of the children of Abraham and their integrity as a chosen nation is the promised Messiah. Without this prospect there is no reason for this nation. We will occupy ourselves with two goals: attack them from without and destroy them from within. Use nearby nations to harass them from without. But more important, distract them from God and create internal decay.

"I adjure you to turn Abraham's children from the memory of God's blessings and care. I intend to personally see that his key offspring have multiple marriages like his. I will make his grandson Israel even more perplexed, causing strife between the many children of his wives. My plan is to induce them to marry while they are very young, before they have the judgment and maturity to choose well, and tempt them with foreign women and their gods. Your place is to help me unify them in violence against their neighbors or in collusion against the few godly among them. Panic them with famine and involve them in wars. Make them greedy for war's spoils and covetous for gold. Distract them and their descendants with women from the nations they conquer. Have them take these godless women for wives, and their gods with them. It will be easy to destroy them from within."

"But," countered Moot, "some of them have God within—"

"I should expect that from you," Lucifer shot back, cutting off his lieutenant.

"I simply was trying to suggest," persisted Moot, "that we must then appear to be as godly as they."

"Well and wisely spoken," Lucifer admitted, and then went on.

"As they throw off restraint and turn from God, see that you have pagan deities ready for them to worship. Many will appreciate gods that they can touch, who require no stretch of faith and whose worship rituals quench their licentious thirst. Carry their sexual appetites into the very act of worship with such gods as Baal and Ashtaroth.

"At planting and harvest times, rationalize sexual intercourse as a beckoning of the gods." Lucifer looked fully now to Ariun. "You, master demon, are good at that. Picture the fertilization of the plants—the deflowering of virgins—as pleasing to the gods. Make them believe that they must keep showing their gods of harvest what to do to begin new growth.

"There will be those whose surrender to us requires something more dramatic. Just as some humans find delight in hunting and killing animals, others will be excited by human sacrifice. I envision a fire god; let's name him Molech. We will impel parents to sacrifice their children to him as part of worship. And social pressure will insure it."

An audible gasp rose from his servants, but Lucifer went on. "They will do it. Oh, their fathers might have recoiled in horror, but we will be dealing with a new generation. Imagine the concept of God this will give them—a cruel, violent God who demands the blood of little children."

He paused, judging his audience's reaction. "That is your chief satanic business, for if they know what God is really like, we lose them.

"The children of men are rapidly multiplying," he added. "And their lifetimes are much shorter than before the flood. The time has come for us to set up a systematic record system. Too long have we relied on our memories and verbal communication. We should take a lesson from heaven and its books of record. We can no longer afford to be concerned with only the present and future. Lessons from the past have much to teach that the present does not know.

"We are already enjoying the fruits of necromancy as people accept our voices as the very voices of the dead. We impersonate their dead friends and loved ones and they welcome us, thus squelching God's warning that separated from Him they will die. We must expand this effort and vigorously utilize our homemade spirits of the dead to satisfy the curiosity of the living. They fear death, those foolish creatures, yet God plans an awakening—a resurrection—for those who have entrusted their lives to Him. Bah!" he spat, "we will cut Him off before He starts. We will convince earth's children that they do not die eternally, but live, whether or not they have trusted their God. We will claim that the death of the human body is a mere transfer into another realm, a greater world.

"Joined with astrology and the occult, this will become a wide-ranging and pervasive philosophy of spiritualism. We will reach the primitive peoples through superstition, and the intellectuals through pseudo-scientific argument, using magic, fear, ridicule and popular appeal. Anyone who turns from us will be viewed as a simple-minded fool. Weaving these cleverly throughout popular religions, people who would be aghast if they understood our intent will happily embrace our message."

"This," spoke up Raa, as Lucifer hesitated, "requires that the evil agent assigned to every human being must be trained to mimic him perfectly."

"Exactly," Lucifer agreed. "For this we must have perfect records of every detail of the lives of the dead—every bias, every appetite, every facial and body nuance, every characteristic and personality quirk, every act—both good and evil—even to the smallest sin. Only then can we as evil spirits fully act out the life of the dead and convince the living that there is a return from the grave.

"I expect each of you to be skillful in this mimicry," he continued, "such clever actors that children will be certain they have seen and talked with their own dead parents. Sweethearts will be impassioned anew with the brief return of their dead lovers. In short, my comrades, we shall convince earth's stupid children that the dead truly live, that death is another of God's lies. Utter confusion will result as religious leaders fondly embrace our travesties.

"But first your commanders must choose from among you those most skilled in *record-keeping*. Beyond establishing your own regional systems, you will share in the building of a master information center so massive in extent and complete in details that each of you has prompt access to every fact in the lives of individuals. Our visual system will be so developed that the file-master and his lieutenants can instantly and completely understand every problem you encounter and collate and coordinate all information, technology and personnel that you require. In fact, I regard this system as of such urgency that I shall personally oversee its establishment and shall regard the file-master as a deputy chief of my staff. Our system and your mastery of its details will provide us a mobility and versatility that will bring down nations."

Excitement sparkled from every eye and gushed through every tongue.

9
MANIPULATING ISRAEL

["Watch," suggested Gabriel, "in the next two showings the cockiness—or should I say *blindness*—of Lucifer, especially when dealing with a young man like Joseph, who is close to God."]

"In the past several centuries we have won many great battles with heaven," Lucifer solemnly began. He had called his commanders together for another executive session. As usual, he expected to plan while they listened and prepared to obey.

"Our counter-intelligence forces are working effectively, and our data system has remarkably strengthened our power to deceive and destroy."

He looked at Gonev. "We have turned the sons of Abraham into enemy clans. We have weakened the Messiah's line by pitting the sons of Isaac against each other and forcing Jacob, the younger, to deceive Esau in order to claim his father's crucial blessing. And we have strewn such jealousies among the diverse sons of Jacob (now called Israel) that their unity is gone, and they have sold their own brother into Egyptian slavery."

Lucifer's confident grin relieved their apprehensions.

"I give you much of the credit," he went on. "Gonev and Queren's work has been brilliant. Nor does that detract from our other efforts," he hurried to add. "Cooperation is the key and it has worked to divide God's chosen nation.

"We—you—have led many of them into early marriages," he chuckled. "They like our philosophy of placing wants before needs. And violence! You are incredible! Israel recoils at Molech's commands and looks down at the poor ignorant pagans who serve him, but Israel's hypocrisy is worse ultimately than the pagans."

He slapped his knee and threw back his head in guttural laughter. "Gonev," he yelled, "you tell us what they've become."

The "stealer" fought to regain his composure, stammering and finally managing to reply. "They are so consumed with greed and passion," he laughed, "that they hardly know where their own tents and purses end and their neighbor's begin."

"They are fascinated with foreign women, too," Queren pointed out, and Lucifer nodded in agreement.

"In fact," Lucifer added, "these women have become such an obsession that God's chosen children are being infected with their godless religions and are bringing their sorceries and pagan rites into Israel's own camp. Murder and rape are commonly practiced. God's people of reformation have become a hallmark of degradation, and we will pursue that decline to the death of the new nation." He waited until the applause of approval died away.

"But how," Lashan challenged Lucifer, "is the camp of Ishmael?"

"We have persuaded him and his descendants to build their own monarchy, contrive their own religions and pursue their own interests with little concern for the God of their father Abraham. Never fear, we will become their gods. At this point the prospect of the Messiah looks increasingly dim. And we have just begun." Again Lucifer paused, acknowledging the applause.

"Yet, as I have insisted before," he went on, "we must never, in deceiving man, allow ourselves the luxury of deception. We made less than an enviable record with Abraham, guided as he had been at times by the physical presence of the angels of heaven who dared to invade our domain. Even the Son himself has at times given personal succor to those whom we have had in our very hands. Abraham's faith on Mount Moriah, his patience with Lot and his repentance for his dalliance with Hagar have done us great harm. Even Isaac has withstood our wiliest temptations, and now if we are not more daring and wise we may lose Jacob, too.

"Already we have ominous reports that his young son Joseph has curried the favor of certain of Pharaoh's high officers. We induced his brothers to sell him to a band of Ishmaelites (see how we are already using Abraham's first son against his people), but I fear we haven't heard the last of his distaste for us."

"So far," grumbled Raa, "Joseph has not yielded to the cleverest of our appeals."

Lucifer winced, and then went on.

"We are further handicapped by the unwillingness of the Deity to allow us to read the minds of men. This is a serious shortcoming in our data bank. We may toy with their principles and sear their consciences, and we may invade their very souls—but only when and if they permit us. Unfortunately, they still have the right of choice which the rest of us sacrificed long ago in the cause of evil." He paused, frowning.

And now Nabal, the chief of staff, spoke up: "We must double our efforts to evaluate all their words and acts, and every mood, expression and circumstance that affects them. Only thus can we fully perceive their lifestyles and understand their minds. We must so arrange their thinking that they assume they are serving God, when in fact they are the best workers we have."

Lucifer agreed: "God has promised earth's children security if they entrust their lives to Him and keep their minds on Him. We must interrupt this thought process in such minds as Joseph's. The Godhead has promised them that if they seek the Three with all their might, they will find them. I find this somewhat mysterious," he mused. "God has implanted in every human being a feeling of incompleteness, a longing for the Three. And you are aware that every person we lose to Him has been drawn to Him by His actually seeking them out. We must obstruct this search for God."

The demons nodded their agreement.

"Women have been among our most efficient tools. We have

been successful in distorting sex from its design as a unique and special bond between a man and a woman. We have made it more of the body than the heart, to the destruction of men and nations. This will be our point of attack on the youth Joseph. In the past we have been satisfied with using almost any woman who would let herself be used. With Joseph we have selected the most beautiful and disarming female in the Egyptian palace, the wife of his master, Potiphar. We need only to trap a man once in such an indiscretion and, consumed with guilt, he will fall at our feet."

"But," interjected Moot, "what if he does not yield?"

"Don't worry, he will," Lucifer promised with a wink.

"He has been very strong," persisted Moot, in whose region Joseph had lived.

"You shall see," predicted Lucifer. "Remember, Moot, your region has become the citadel of our strength. One young man can hardly be considered a threat. He'll never stand."

"I hope—" Moot began, but was interrupted by his master.

"I have commended your general manipulation of the Israelite nation, yet some of you are guilty of inexcusable stupidity and dereliction in the handling of young Joseph at the pit. His brothers were jealous and angry enough to kill him on the spot. You had many alternatives—killing him earlier, diverting Judah from his rescue, and devising a more believable tale to tell to old man Israel. It would be better for our purpose if the lad were dead. Israel still does not trust his sons, except for the youngest—who, of course, does not know what his brothers did to Joseph."

"Master," intruded Gonev, "we did our very best with Joseph."

Lucifer looked at "the stealer" with narrowed eyes and demanded, "Then your best will have to be better." Pausing to let the words sink in, he went on.

"I am—with your help, of course—developing both short- and long-range plans for the desecration of Israel and the obstruction of the messianic plan. Both are directly under the governance of heaven. However, we must not permit such a theocracy to survive. Even though it is a lesser government-by-

God than the Eden plan, it poses uncertainties for us as long as we cannot read the minds of men nor always correctly discern the messages of God to men. As of now, God's nation, weak though it is, still recognizes God as its Head. Sooner or later, we will manipulate Israel's government into the hands of men. We will substitute men as judges and eventually as kings. This will separate, as far as possible, God's rule from His nation on earth.

"Meanwhile, Moot, we must have an alternative for Joseph in the unlikely event that the woman fails."

The somber demon nodded dutifully.

"Let us devise a world famine of such devastating proportions that man—even Israel—must cry out against God. And in the uncertainty of the nations, Israel will be vulnerable for blame. This small nation has already made itself a stench before its neighbors with its record of rampant violence—even massacres—and of sexual license. Judah's daughter-in-law, Tamar, was forced to pose as a prostitute to earn what was rightfully hers, and the heinous behavior of Israel's sons over the rape of Dinah still echoes in surrounding nations.

"Indeed, you have done your devilish best in that family. Yet that must be exceeded if I read the signs of Joseph well. Every data bit handed me from our information center piles higher the evidence that we have a dangerous challenge before us. I do not flinch from danger, as you know, but we all have reason to fear the unknown in the mind of a godly man."

"Please be specific then," spoke Raa in support of Gonev. Lucifer was irritated.

"By following famine with oppression for the Israelite nation, providing a sequence of Pharaohs and kings of extreme cruelty, we can force them to forget their God. We will make them slaves who are forced to sweat for their own water and beg for their food. See that they are whipped, even as they build cities to our pagan inventions. Give them quotas, and when they complain of cruelty and futility, see that they are forced to produce more out of less, even to make bricks without straw.

"God will, of course, interfere. But He must work within the limits of the divine commitment to give man choice. No matter how powerful He is, His love gives Him no alternative. So we must accuse Him and devastate Him before the universe, protesting His unreasonable protection over His 'saints' as a violation of His word. We will test Him until He writhes on His throne."

10
THE EGYPTIAN FIASCO

The next change in the panorama showed that Lucifer and his staff chief, Nabal, had once again sent out word for a meeting of leading officers in his great council room.

"I have called you here today to commend and to warn. Your growing oppression of Israel in Goshen has been notable, but your handling first of Thutmose III and his exile of Moses was extraordinary. Those of you who were at the palace observed the surprise on the courtiers' faces when Moses returned from his forty-year exile in the wilderness. The Pharaoh's magicians duplicated the feat of Aaron, Moses' brother, of turning his staff into a serpent. Yet we must face the serious culmination of that meeting—Moses' serpent swallowing all the snakes of the Pharaoh's men and then transforming itself back into a staff again." He frowned. Then, his voice rolling like thunder, he continued. "That act has ominous overtones for us.

"We moved well with the Pharaoh through all God's plagues except for the death decree. Though each plague attacked the power of a different Egyptian god, we still maintained their confidence. Afterward, we aroused the King to pursue the fleeing Israelites. But in retrospect, I am not pleased that we set up a confrontation at the Red Sea. For us that was a disaster far more serious than most of you admit.

"It had taken us centuries to develop the fullness of our reign in and through Egypt. Wielding together religion and politics, we had made the pharaohs the most feared men on earth.

And the refinement of magic coupled with medicine made for awesome control of the people through the priesthood. This was the pinnacle of our achievements—yet God could tear these apart and foil our program with one man's obedience. Disgusting! You're all disgusting! We have lost the advantage and the nation is on the verge of unlocking our lies! We must move to cause Israel to forget that victory and to malign the man Moses. And our attention must go back to the reason why we lost both Moses and Joseph."

Lucifer tapped on the podium impatiently. "It is of utmost importance that we so preoccupy this people with daily cares that they feel they do not have time for God. And we must instill this indifference to God from early childhood.

"We were incautious with Joseph as a boy. No, I am not accusing you. But our stupidity cost us the man—a monumental loss."

Moot was careful not to make a point of his prediction, and Lucifer avoided his gaze as he went on.

"Though Potiphar's wife tried to seduce him day after day, he never weakened. We failed to see that the decision was not made in those moments, but years before when he determined to follow God's way at any cost. Moot was right..."

The somber demon lowered his head at the master's compliment.

Lucifer continued. "We lost Joseph long before that final attack—when spurned, the woman accused him of rape—and therein lies the problem. It is imperative that we conquer these people while they are children.

"We likewise lost Moses when we failed to distract his mother and sister sufficiently. Never forget that those first ten or twelve years of life are crucial to us in deforming their characters. We relaxed when Pharaoh's daughter found Moses in his basket in the bulrushes. We thought Egyptian education would draw him to us, but his mother's influence was stronger." He grimaced.

Rasha looked skeptically at him, but Lucifer avoided his eyes.

"We dare never to relax," he continued. "I tell you again,

we must never rest!" He pounded the podium. "We shall divert, but we must never be diverted. We shall deceive, but we must never be fooled! With both Joseph and Moses *we were fools.*"

"Who is the real fool?" Rasha angrily whispered to Raa.

Lucifer did not notice: "Now God has put His miserable Law on stone! It does not take careful study to see that this Law reflects God's character. He has clearly designed it to be a safeguard for those who follow Him and an obstacle for those who obey us. It is absolutely necessary that the children of Israel see these commands as despotic demands. They must not understand them as principles of love."

"But remember," reminded Moot, "you are dealing with the character of God. Perhaps we should be cautious—"

"Teach them to take the names of Deity in vain," spat Lucifer. "Mix their language with minced oaths. Urge them on to scorn and ridicule any phrase that describes God's character: 'Gracious, Goodness and so on.' Lead them to be so unaware of God's glory that they use His name in the same breath they damn their enemies. See that they rationalize all manner of violations, even ignoring the needs and honor of their parents. When parents grow old, cause their children to consider them useless and let others care for them."

The demons nodded, grinning—even Raa, Rasha and Moot.

"You remember at Eden that God set aside one whole day of every week for His creatures to meet with Him and claimed to make that day holy. He now states in the fourth commandment that He set it apart for holy use from the beginning in order to be even more personally involved with them. Now He even has gone so far as to write it with His own finger in tablets of stone, placing it in the center of His set of moral laws. Furthermore, that commandment identifies the Creator of heaven and earth. We must combat this. You will take care to desecrate His Sabbath day at every turn. Where you cannot make people wholly forget it, see that they give God only the briefest nod and use the rest of the day for themselves more than in service to others. Where you cannot do this, teach man to make it a day of rigid exactions rather than love for God."

"Just how," demanded Raa, "do you propose to do this?"

For a moment, Lucifer glared at him impatiently, then began slowly.

"Israel is now a rich people," he said, changing the subject. "In fear and despair, after the deaths of their firstborn, the Egyptians threw their jewels at the Israelites, so desperate were they to rid Egypt of that hated people. We can utilize this new wealth as a stumbling block to them so they fondly recall Egypt as a land of plenty rather than remembering their oppression. Our taunts will follow them as they wander in the desert—laughing that they worship a wilderness God who has deserted them when they need Him most.

"Point out to them the prosperity of the wicked and challenge their reasons for ignoring the joys of sin. Obsess them with the conviction that possessions and fame are the measure of success, thereby making them less thankful than demanding of their Father. The desert sun will suck dry their body fluids until they blaspheme Him and damn the day they accepted His leading. Then we have them, making them demons like you and me." Lucifer uttered a guttural laugh.

There was a smattering of applause.

"But," he continued, "we must be alert for a certain faith in God among them, and crush it at all costs. I speak again of such as the spirit of Joseph and Moses and Aaron and now Caleb and Joshua . . . and their predecessor, Job.

"That man gave me more personal trouble than I like to remember. As I promised you, I personally challenged the Godhead for overprotecting their creatures. I accused them of violating the very gift of choice, and used Job as an example. But our plans went awry." His voice hardened. "We had not taken sufficient time to preoccupy him and his family with the cares of their lives, and no matter what I did to him, he never stopped trusting God.

"Yet this experience has taught us another fundamental principle: the diabolical keenness of the tool of accusation. Each of Job's friends, under stress, turned out to be an accuser. We must make all people quick to accuse without fact and, if the accusations happen to be true, to keep up their charges until they have destroyed the accused ones' influence and reputation.

Since man is so aware of himself, and since self-worth is so basic to his sociability and success, we must spare no effort to poison his neighbors' tongues.

"Let us use his concern for the approval of his peers as one of the surest avenues to our hellish sanctum. The lessons of Joseph, Moses, and even of Abel and Cain long before, teach us that we must extend these pressures into childhood. We must do everything in our darkest power to divest the patriarchal family of its potential for good. We shall use every plague of darkness to relax the parents and turn their sense of responsibility into surrender to their offspring's clamor for freedom. We dare not rest until we have made the values of every child less dependent upon his family than his peers, and the values of every family more centered in themselves than in their God. We will make the children of God into sons of devils."

The words "Well spoken," "Yea, Yea," and "Wise, indeed" could be heard across the room. Then Lucifer went on.

"Doing this, they will make increasing demands of the Deity without meeting His conditions of obedience. As the parents demonstrate their disobedience before their offspring, the children will correctly see and assess them as hypocrites. And since God planned that every parent should be the example of God to his child until the age of reason, we will give the young ones a distorted idea of God. That is our goal! I have already begun with the sons of Aaron.

"Review carefully these admonitions." Lucifer's voice, now soft and lyrical, had a hypnotizing quality. "Oppression, depression, possession; accusation, hypocrisy, confusion. And the earlier the age that we reach them, the more certain we are to control them. Remember," he concluded, "the devil-kept are the God-denied."

11
SUBSTITUTING FOR THE GOVERNMENT OF GOD

The screen now brightened with another council scene. Lucifer's smile embraced the throng, making each of his followers feel needed and successful.

"Today I am happy to confirm what you already know: We have now completely confounded the Godhead's plans for a theocracy on earth." He paused, smiling a thank-you to the applause.

"We successfully induced Israel to demand a king—like their pagan neighbors. Israel chose to be ruled by these kings—men placed between their nation and God. This interposes human wisdom in all the nation's transactions between God and man. Our plan was eventually to flog their kingdom with wars from without and to divide it by internal dissension until it destroys itself as the nation of God.

"Yet we have reason to reflect. I shudder when I recall Joshua's challenge to Israel to 'choose you this day whom ye will serve, but as for me and my house, we will serve the Lord.' The sheer fortitude of this man has been a cloud of rejection which still mars our horizon. I warn you to study every family in Israel for offspring who appear to be leaders. Recruit them cleverly, tactfully but firmly pressing them into our service from their earliest years.

"You failed—I failed—with Joshua. He showed so little promise of leadership as a boy." He frowned, continuing in a puzzled tone. "They still have the power to choose God and to resist us."

"God helps them," Herev spoke up.

"But why?" Lashan countered.

Lucifer raised his eyebrows at such free discussion. "Lashan?"

The "tongue" stood up. "I am wondering why out of the million and more Israelites who left Egypt, only a handful didn't die before reaching Canaan? If we succeeded with all of them, where did we fail with Joshua and Caleb and Moses?"

"Such discussion is good," Lucifer told him. "As to the reason, that is for you to study further. To win, we must destroy the Joshuas *before* they cripple us."

Lashan nodded. "Of course," he replied.

"Now," Lucifer went on, "Israel followed our schedule in her rejection of the Deity. Her rise and fall as a nation of God looked like an endless chain of mountain peaks. Each time she turned from the Creator in presumption, she embarrassed Him and fell prey to the heathen armies about her. She finally pled to God in desperation and He sent His judge to restore her. She then rose again, but seldom as high as before. Like gullible fools on their successive highs and lows, the nation deteriorated in every new phase. And as the mountain chain narrows and dims in the distance, so the future of national Israel will one day disappear.

"You have done well consuming the Israelite mind with pride in every point where humility should have reigned. You have insidiously taught them that to be humble is humiliating and to be intellectual is wise." He smiled. "As they pit their wisdom against divinity, they turn into more effective agents of darkness than the pagans around them.

"You defiled well the sons of the high priest Eli. Their flirtation with the fertility rites of the Canaanites is still the talk of Israel—a tantalizing whisper for every Israelite daughter and a demonic model for every Israelite son." The demons chuckled.

"Midbar," Lucifer called, "what is our overall goal?"

Midbar blinked, grabbing his thoughts. "Our goal is to discredit God," he replied. "We must never let people know what He is really like."

"Well said," Lucifer intoned, "and we are doing very well. And you outdid yourself in stealing the sons of the saintly Samuel, whom God used to storm our satanic citadel as the 'perfect' child."

"Yes," laughed Raa, "that was a slap in God's face!"

Lucifer joined him in laughter. "You will recall how, as a child, Samuel stupidly criticized Eli's sons to his face in the name of God. The joke is that he grew so busy doing the work of God, he didn't take time to protect his children from us. Such techniques are superb, and your shafts well aimed.

"Let this be a lesson to all demon hosts in every nether region," he declared, waving his hand, palm out. "It is crucial that you preoccupy all parents in your care with demonic disappointments or delights. It matters not which you choose as long as you suit the device to the task. I don't care whether parents are obsessed with the work of God or are fascinated with themselves. Simply be certain that they are bent more on their daily cares and amusements than on the rearing of their children. Drive them to coolness and inconsistency. So tool their responses and their freedoms that they become inattentive to the emerging needs of their young.

"Selfishness grows best in the guise of love. Make love's counterfeit clever and sure. You are learning well the art of taming the wild demands of God.

"Yet, with all this optimism, I must pose some sobering thoughts." He leaned upon his desk—his long fingers forming a pyramid with his thumbs. "Take Judge Samson, for example. I am vexed by his eventual desertion of our camp in spite of our mastery. Why was an alert not sounded? It was clear that Samson's luxuriant hair was a symbol of the man's trust in divine power. When he gave up his secret to Delilah and she shaved his head, he voluntarily separated himself from God and, as we expected, God took away his strength."

"Perhaps we were incautious in blinding him," suggested Midbar.

"Understated," applauded Lucifer. "We were impetuous.

Samson, of course, had qualms of conscience when he found himself in Delilah's power. And when we took his eyes, his anger turned on us. Alone, imprisoned, his mind turned back to God. And God forgave the wretch. We should have watched keenly his every move, to discern his intentions—which God already knew. (I assumed that we had learned this lesson long ago from the reform of the prostitute Rahab.) So the sum of the power Samson displayed when he died was greater than all his life, and he carried our best Philistine servants with him to death. In the name of deceit and damnation, this must never happen again!"

"But let's not forget," interjected Skahor, "that we are dealing with a God who knows our every thought."

Lucifer paled for a moment. Then he went on, his tone now accusing: "And there are many of you who wish you had never heard the name of Gideon.

"Here was a lackey whom you ignored—threshing grain in a wine press to hide it from the Midianites. But you underestimated God's ability to use such a weakling. His faith you perceived as folly, and his hesitancy as a coward's cloak. But he took 300 men against the hosts of Midian and destroyed our finest human army! Years of work destroyed by their deceiving—they stole a page from our book! If you see fire in my eyes," he shouted, "understand that there is satanic reason!" Heads in the circle again raised to snatch a look at their leader.

"Why," demanded Raa, "do you accuse us? You are the chief devil!"

"You heard what I said, 'evil devil,' " retorted Lucifer.

"Indeed," flaunted Raa, while all others except Rasha hung their heads.

"I will take the responsibility," conceded Lucifer, and continued. "All is not lost if, from now on, we induce men, like Gideon, to demand miraculous 'signs' in determining God's will. Then they will depend less on prayer and study of His previous word to them. Rather, we will urge them to insist on signs and, more deviously, to suggest to Him what these signs shall be. By limiting the response of God, they will drift into an indifferent and demanding relationship with Him."

"Yes," agreed Nabal, the staff chief, "we do not care how the sign comes out so long as the 'sign' limits God to the boundaries men set, no matter how absurd. And why shouldn't we manipulate those signs? We can create changes in weather; we can give dreams to the sons of Israel; we can induce prophets to prophesy falsely. We can induce illness . . ."

Lashan seconded Nabal, but Rasha had some questions on his mind.

"It seems to me we should expect God to reverse the ravages of sin occasionally, and we may expect Him to heal diseases at the requests of His friends. What do you suggest then?"

Lucifer looked straight at Rasha, his eyes narrowed to slits. "We will counterfeit such miracles and confuse people, particularly when the healings appear to come through the prayers of those whose lives obviously follow our way. By taking away sickness we have created and glorifying the hypocrites' prayers, we will laugh in the face of God."

[Gabriel smiled sadly as he commented on our enemy's words. "Lucifer enjoys lashing out with a statement like that," he told me. "And indeed, they have laughed—and spit in our Father's face.

"The years passed," continued Gabriel, "Lucifer's success mounted. The children of God's nation chose to be ruled by a king, like their pagan neighbors."]

Lucifer was triumphant. He had worked hard to reach this goal.

"God," he exulted, "did not hide His reluctance to see Israel ruled by kings. I think He fears that they will usurp His power. Be sure you suggest to men that He considers them insignificant, all the while claiming to lead them like a shepherd. Describe Him more as the lion that devours the sheep than the master herdsman He pretends to be. Is not God, rather than I, the adder with the deadly sting? When He is seen as a devil, we will be perceived as gods."

"Well said," spoke several commanders as one.

"We began well with King Saul," Lucifer went on. "If there

had to be a king, he was to be one of God's making—tall, generous, and noble; powerful, courageous and wise." His mouth twisted barbarously.

"Yes, God gave him a new heart," laughed Nabal.

"Yet," grinned Lucifer, "we turned him into a jealous, self-serving maniac who feared his own shadow and who came to us on his knees: His approach to our agent, the witch at Endor, was that of a groveling fool. And he died by his own hand!"

His comrades howled, jostling each other, remembering the ridiculous spectacle.

"Indeed such deceptions are amusing to us," Lucifer continued, "and you are to be commended. The tearing asunder of David's kingdom was nearly flawless. Your record with the kings of the Northern Kingdom remained unscathed and its fall to Sargon the Assyrian was masterful. Many promotions are being processed now because of our phenomenal success of inculcating impurity and idolatry into the worship of Israel. King Ahab and our charming Jezebel were mighty instruments of corruption.

"The deportation of the best of the Northern Kingdom and the repopulating of their land with captives from Elam and Babylonia may prove to be of great consequence. The intermarriage of the Jews remaining in the land and the foreigners to form the racial group called the Samaritans is another schism in Israel we will use to exploit. The hatred we can develop among the true Jews towards them is limitless. Make sure they fully mix their foreign idolatry with the Jewish Law. Raise up a center for worship there, make sure they include the books of Moses, and establish a priesthood that will mirror that of Jerusalem. Move it as close as possible to the established worship of God while retaining as much idolatry as possible. Sow seeds of enmity between them and the Jews in Judah until they become a source of continual racial prejudice. Religious hatred: who would have thought it to be one of our strongest weapons!

"Thanks to your hard efforts and willing servants in Assyria we have little to worry about concerning the ten 'lost' tribes."

Now Lucifer arose from his desk. His mood suddenly darkened. He seemed deeply agitated as he spoke.

"There are several names on my records which do not reflect genius on you and me, and which, like Enoch, Moses, and Joshua, have been a threat to my kingdom. Have any of you forgotten how Jonah escaped our doom and wreaked havoc in our central base of operation? How is this possible? And what about the prophets Elijah and Elisha and of the kings Josiah and Hezekiah? You had Elijah in your very hands and let him go. I will never forget the loss of those 450 prophets of Baal—the choicest among our sensuous clergy."

"Who let him go?" demanded Raa. Lucifer understood and went on.

"Nor have I ever been more embarrassed than when God blinded the great Assyrian army in answer to Elisha's prayer. Then, to compound the humiliation, Elisha led the sightless enemy soldiers into the fortress of his own king." He gritted his teeth. "And I fear most of all the God-given courage of such youths as King Josiah."

The demon officers nodded. They clearly agreed.

"Remember how, at the tender age of 20, he set out to destroy all our gods within the borders of Israel and tore down every idol grove. Most notorious of all, he turned the hearts of Israel to heaven. And even the foolish Hezekiah so claimed the Godhead's power when attacked by the Assyrians that God sent an angel who destroyed the enemy army. If you had not manipulated the kings that followed, we might have been destroyed by now."

The demons were grateful for even a wisp of gratitude.

"I charge you to attack the prophets of Israel," Lucifer roared. "They serve only to disrupt us. Use all your cleverness to counter the ministry of Jeremiah. Especially confuse and confound those who read Isaiah's work with his obsession for the poor and the needy and the eternal Sabbath and the promised Messiah. Give all the prophets and priests and leaders a sense of power, but make it empty power. Since their only real strength against us comes from God, you must divert them from intimacy with the Trinity. And multiply the numbers of those who speak our message in God's name. Make numbers more significant than faith."

Nabal spoke up again.

"These servants of God are bent on making everyone a minister, challenging all to be watchmen and shepherds. This we should fiercely oppose."

"I order you to make certain," Lucifer replied, "that these people continually study God's Word but never come to know what He is really like. Fiercely, at all costs with any and all devices, make sure that they hear but do not understand; that they see, but do not perceive. See that they are confused, certain that they are wise and uncertain of God's wisdom. Thus they may forfeit their salvation."

"Some of our team," volunteered Raa, "have been making a special study of the prophets."

"Yes, tell us," invited Lucifer.

"As I see it," Raa said, "Isaiah described the coming of the Messiah in enough detail to be uncomfortable to us. He foretells that Christ will come as a tender plant, with no comeliness nor beauty—as a meek and humble servant. And this must be true."

"Exactly," agreed Lucifer. "It is a brilliant and devious device of God which He is compelled to implement if He carries out His pretense of grace and love."

"Then what do you suggest?" inquired Rasha skeptically.

"You are," instructed Lucifer, "to instill into the very corners of man's consciousness that his Redeemer is to come as a bejeweled King, conquering and to conquer. Assure the Israelites that their Savior must overwhelm the enemy by sheer military might. Move them to ignore the prophets' prediction that He is to be a man of sorrows and persuade them to hold tenaciously onto their dream that the Messiah will conquer by force, as a warrior chief acquainted more with power than with grief."

Rasha, Raa and the commanders nodded in agreement.

"We shall indeed," concluded Lucifer, "see that the Messiah is despised and rejected. We will give the Godhead a ghoulish model of humility in His chosen people. Our design is to make them kill the King He sends to save them!"

12
THE BABYLONIAN THREAT

["Lucifer lays his plans well, *very* well," Gabriel told me, "then carries them out systematically. His followers, the fallen angels, almost stumble over themselves to carry out his commands. And they do so with great efficiency.

"His goal at this point was to make the city of Babylon into a world empire—an empire which would swallow God's children as a walrus devours a baby seal."

"But you say God allowed it," I protested. "Why does God allow such horror?"

"Ah, my friend, you miss the point," Gabriel replied gently. "If God's chosen people had allowed Him to lead and protect them, not even the combined efforts of every angel in hell could have harmed one of them." His face conveyed infinite sadness. "Oh, a few were faithful to their Father, but as a nation Judah callously turned away from Him as Israel had done before. God allowed the terrors and the unspeakable tragedies they endured in Babylonian captivity as a way to guide them back to Him."

"Those who are separated from God will die," I sighed.

And Gabriel agreed softly, "Just as God warned your first parents. Yet centuries passed and still His children were unconvinced."

Then the panorama was again spread out before me.]

The demons gave their leader a standing ovation as he entered the great hall and took his place at the podium. He stood silently for a long moment, basking in their adoration. It was a smaller group that awaited his message this time, a mere fraction of his satanic multitude. Only commanders and their deputies had been summoned, and a few whose recent work merited special honor.

"Greetings again, fellow princes of darkness. I can truly call you princes. There is no infantry so warlike, there are no charioteers so eager, and there is no angel host so devoted and ruthlessly efficient in deceit and destruction as you—the elite who stand before me tonight." His words resounded against the burnished walls. "It gives me great fulfillment to be your commander.

"I trust that it is thrilling to you that our powerful and pagan Babylon has overwhelmed the fawning offspring of God. The children of Israel—hypocrites of your making—have fallen like masochistic pigs before our swordsmen."

The demons laughed and clapped like excited children. "In a spelling out of horrors, God's chosen people literally destroyed themselves—even at last devouring their own little children. The pitiful few who remain now wail over the memory of Jerusalem under the willows on the banks of old Eden's Euphrates." He laughed. "It is now our Babylon's favorite river. These 'children of God,' these braggarts of heaven, who claimed the Deity's continual protection, are pinned like squirming insects under the darkest shadows of your wings.

"Our manipulation of Solomon is now old history, but his example still lives on to contradict his famed works of wisdom. We have skillfully used leader after leader to transform the children of Judah into worshipers of Baal. The legacy of King Manasseh and those like him has opened wide the doors for their massacre by Nebuchadnezzar of Babylon. The sons of the fickle Zedekiah were slain before his eyes—eyes then ripped out by Babylon's generals." Lucifer threw back his head and laughed again. "What a remarkable picture of the king of God's chosen people!"

"Yet," he began, and then his expression changed. The pause grew long, as though he pondered a deep mystery. "I sometimes have a feeling in my inward parts that God is toying with us. It appears that those who love Him die when He decides their work is done, and He seals them for eternity. These die with His assurance of eventual bodily resurrection. It is imperative that we candidly face the divine reasoning and plan accordingly, lest the Deity make us appear as fools before the universe and confirm our damnation. I fear God speaks the truth when He says that for those who die trusting Him, their centuries of dreamless 'sleep' will seem but an eyeblink when their Father recreates them in the promised image of God. We must twist this promise into a lie.

"But take care! It does not help our mission to ignore the hand of God. Bear vividly in mind how He wiped out 185,000 of Sennacherib's select Assyrian swordsmen in a moment's time. That attack verifies the harshness of the divine power we face. If God's people begin to take hold of the Father, we know the consequences. While this is no time for discouragement"—he spoke very slowly, emphasizing each word—"I talk seriously to you tonight that you may be stirred to a more heroic defiance of the Three than you have yet imagined.

"We need a greater effort than we have made thus far if we are to overpower Daniel, the young Hebrew in Babylon.

"Lashan," he called to the "tongue," "which of our enemies does this Daniel remind you of?"

Lashan stood facing his leader, proud to respond. "Abel and Joseph, perhaps, and"—he cleared his throat—"oh, and Moses and Elijah."

Lucifer nodded. "Well said, my prince. I would say that this Daniel has all the offensive traits of these men blended into one. His hand is firmly placed in God's, and he consistently walks with Him. We must use every device imaginable to sidetrack or even kill him. He must *not* continue this role!

"You did well at first in reducing him to slavery." Lucifer smiled slightly, then became somber. "But his influence on his Hebrew colleagues became so powerful they all faced death rather than eat the rich palace foods and drink the liquors of the court. And he came out of that experiment ten times wiser than all of our astrologers and magicians."

Suddenly Lucifer became flushed at the thought. He pounded his fist against the podium.

"Where were you in all of this?" he screamed. "Your most diabolical efforts were less than a gentle breeze against this rock of a man." A deathly hush, broken only by a few nervous coughs, fell over the throng. No one dared raise his head except Lashan, the "tongue."

"What would you like us to do that we could manage?" Lashan asked, as if innocent.

Lucifer was furious. Then his anger seemed to subside. Ignoring Lashan for the moment, he said, "When King Nebuchadnezzar was troubled by forgetting his dream, not one astrologer or sorcerer or Chaldean wise man in all the Babylonian courts could recall it for him." He leaned forward, his low, deliberate speech more terrifying than his shouts. "I sometimes wonder if you have any brains in your heads or are too cowardly to use them!" he hissed.

"This entire affair has been an acute embarrassment to me. How is it that our headquarters has again been attacked from within?" Lucifer looked straight at Lashan as though he were the culprit, then slowly covered all with his gaze as if to cast a spell.

"Daniel," he continued slowly, "waited until the most propitious moment to make his entry before the king, and then did not come in the vanity and elegance for which our wise men are known. Oh, no. He came in meekness and humility!" Lucifer trembled. "I can hardly stand the sight of that man!"

The multitude sank even lower in their chairs.

"Observe the mastery of that young Hebrew," Lucifer went on. "His behavior makes me shudder, yet we can learn much from it. He boldly told the king that he wanted no gifts, scorning the very riches that had our wise men agog. He was cool and composed when they were frantic, even though he knew he was condemned to die with our men—who could not retrieve the dream. He simply insisted on a quiet time with his God who was despised by the king and his court."

"But just what would you suggest we do?" Lashan persisted.

Lucifer ignored him and continued his ranting. "Where does he get his peace?" he screamed. "Our wise men were witless in their terror!"

No one answered, not even Lashan or Raa. Indeed, Lucifer did not expect a reply. His own voice betrayed his amazement.

"And then Daniel came back to tell the king's dream in every explicit and startling detail. So what do we have now? An indifferent, helpless slave working under the prince of eunuchs, behind the scenes in the palace? No, the king made him prime minister of the realm! And get this: the king bowed flat on his face before that young Jew! He even acknowledged Daniel's God as the 'God of gods.'" Lucifer whirled, throwing up both arms as if in despair.

"Even more ominous to us," he shrieked, "you may be sure that Daniel's story will be recorded in the Jewish Scriptures, as an example for others to read! I tell you, I charge you, get rid of not only this man but also the Scriptures that God insists on having His people record. Destroy every page, mutilate every scroll, lest others use them as Josiah did to turn the people against us.

"Some of you saw what happened on the plain of Dura. The infection of those three men by Daniel's spirit accounts well for their defiance of Nebuchadnezzar when they were ordered to worship him. That great statue of the king should have struck them with reverence and awe. It was ninety feet high and made of gold, yet they refused even to bow their heads. So the furious king directed that they be thrown into the fiery furnace, heated seven times hotter than usual. And what happened? Raa, what happened?"

"The overpowering heat killed the guards who threw them into the furnace," replied Raa, almost stoically.

"And then what?" Lucifer demanded impatiently.

"The ropes were burned off the captives, but they weren't even singed."

"Out with it!" Lucifer bellowed.

"The Son of God appeared with the three in the fire."

"That," groaned Lucifer, "astonished even me—that He would come down from heaven for so mere an event.

"Of course the king was awed!" he hissed. "Who wouldn't be? When he saw the burned ropes but not even a hair singed, he was scared. Who wouldn't be in the face of such power? And when he called them out of the flames, they did not even have the smell of fire on them! So what did Nebuchadnezzar do but *promote* the Hebrews and order all in his kingdom to reverence their God. Our man defied us instead of the Trinity!"

"And he is becoming one of them!" Moot interrupted.

Lucifer turned on him angrily. "I need not tell you that I will permit no more disasters like this! He was a fully trained idolater and the most powerful man in the world."

"Perhaps," added Nabal, "it is time to give closer attention to the signals of God if we are to turn events."

"Yes," agreed Lashan. "Nebuchadnezzar's first dream of the strange image has great significance for us."

Lucifer looked at him curiously, but Lashan went on.

"Since that statue's materials clearly predict the world powers of future centuries and hint that after Rome there shall be a great breakdown among the world powers before the final advent of Christ, we might do well to reevaluate our strategy."

"Take care," flashed Lucifer. "We plan the disruption of every prophecy, whether it concerns nations or men or the Son himself. Let us scar the Babylonian image's golden head and cut down the Medo-Persian breast and arms of silver; let us pollute the Grecian belly and thighs of brass and destroy with the Roman legs of iron; and we must then form other world powers. We defy the disruptive prophecy of the iron and clay in the image's feet. We still have every option open to us—wars and intrigue and even intermarriage among kingdoms—to weld the nations together.

"Our first defiant step is the total degradation of Babylon. If the Deity is determined to set up and destroy nations, we will cooperate, as I said before. But it will be done in our own way!"

"I want to see this," spat Rasha to Raa. Lucifer did not seem to hear.

"I have often directed your mind to His Word," Lucifer reminded, "specifically to the scrolls of Isaiah and his predictions that Cyrus the Persian will conquer Babylon. I planned that you destroy him as a child, but you were unable to touch him. When his grandfather desired his death, you allowed him to be spirited away to the country. And now he is emerging as commander of the Persian hordes. If you still cannot kill him, I charge you to destroy him from within. Do your fiendish best to turn the predictions of Isaiah to nonsense."

"Please tell us," asked the agitated Rasha, "how to get around the prophecy."

"I am determined to contradict the words of the prophet directly. You must not allow Cyrus to do a 'Nebuchadnezzar' on us. If you are able to change the Cyrus prophecy in the slightest detail, I will heap honors upon you."

The demons showed more skepticism than anticipation, but Lucifer continued.

"Isaiah has even daringly prophesied that Babylon's gates would be left open, and he has even described which gates. He naively predicted that eventually Babylon will be so demolished that it will never be rebuilt. Yet he predicted that *Cyrus* would lead in the *rebuilding* of Jerusalem! Imagine! One of our men building their city!"

It was now Raa's turn to interrupt. "What new idea do you propose?"

The master was quick to answer. "We must contend with the fact that the Godhead knows the innermost secrets of man's conscience and the intricate details of the future. This has been an overriding handicap to us which we must turn aside. So I am instructing you to see that any foreknowledge of God is perceived as predestination so people believe He sets men up only to strike them down and that He gleefully thrives on the suffering of His created beings. You must insure that all three of the Trinity are feared as cruel and arbitrary and determined to use their creatures as robots which they can manipulate to satisfy their own sadistic ends.

"We now will also carry out more completely our carefully laid plans to counterfeit the Trinity."

The demons straightened, clearly hoping for a creative idea.

"First, we have long elevated Nimrod, our first pagan king, as a surrogate Father. This evil and powerful monarch, this hunter of hunters, set a diabolical example after the flood by building his Tower of Babel in the plains of Shinar. Even the children of God are mystified at his influence and power in the Mesopotamian Valley. And we will puzzle them more.

"Second, we will name the early Babylonian King Tammuz as the false Son of God. He is our 'son of life'—the god of fertility and harvest. We will make the women of Israel weep more for Tammuz than for the Son.

"Third, we have the ideal substitute for the Holy Spirit in the sensual Semiramis. This mythical Assyrian goddess will be a perfect counterfeit for the Third Person of the Godhead. You have done well in creating the story of her mysterious vanishing from the earth as a dove—the divine characterization of the Holy Spirit. We will issue from her a total worship of the senses, which will become central to those who claim theirs are the true religions.

"Finally, we must move to do all within our power to hinder the latest of the messages being circulated from God's prophets. While Daniel's testimony has resulted in much of the world hearing about the Father, Ezekiel and Jeremiah have been far too busy and their message has spread like wildfire. Going to Egypt has no more shut up Jeremiah than hauling Ezekiel to the River Chebar. Their messages are far too clear, and Jeremiah's precise message concerning the seventy years could prevent the solidifying of our despair over these people. This message must not be allowed to spread! Do all in your power to dissolve the faith of the faithful and fill them with such doubt and skepticism about the unseen as to obliterate any belief they may have in the goodness of God."

The demons responded with a standing ovation.

"Then," concluded Lucifer, relishing the rare emotional high of the moment, "then we will become their gods!"

The great hall resounded with their laughter and applause.

13
THE STRANGE DOINGS OF CYRUS THE PERSIAN

There was something different about the next scene. As it began, Lucifer raised his hand half-heartedly to the ovation by his assembled officers. Once again he had summoned only top leaders.

"As much as I acknowledge your loyalty, I am not in the mood for applause tonight. While I am fully aware of your unceasing busyness, I am also convinced of the activity of our enemy, God. I do not speak casually to you this evening about Him.

"I am bitterly disappointed in our Babylon record." Lucifer now frowned. "Indeed, we made King Belshazzar into a drunken sot and turned his miserable court into a jungle of sensuous beasts. And yes, we tore Babylon's golden empire to pieces. Yet heaven confounded our major steps: Nebuchadnezzar's first dream embarrassed our astrologers and magicians and brought the king to his knees before God. The result of his threats to Daniel's three companions made him again bend low in awe of heaven's power. And the later fulfillment of his second dream was a slap in our faces: His temporary insanity actually led our pagan king finally to become our enemy—a worshiper of God."

Lucifer pulled a cord, and draperies slid silently aside, leaving a pale, glimmering wall. He nodded to Nabal, who focused a powerful projector on that wall. At the touch of Lucifer's finger, the hall became alive with color and sound. (He always insisted that everything be at his finger's touch, and went into a rage at the slightest failure. But this time all was well prepared.)

The commanders watched, fascinated, as they viewed the drunken Belshazzar at his last feast. They saw a disembodied hand writing on the banquet room wall—words that sealed the king's fate. Some demons turned away momentarily at the sight of the stupefied Belshazzar and his courtiers, frozen with fear.

The scene changed. King Cyrus diverted the river. ("An action so close to prophecy that one might think Isaiah had been there watching 150 years before," Lucifer noted bitterly, alluding to Isaiah 44 and 45.)

The group watched Cyrus climbing the wall above the riverbed to the gates left open and unguarded for the first time in a century. They were fascinated as the great general and his army stormed the city and poured into the banquet hall. With a hand now unsteady, Lucifer turned off the machine.

No one spoke. Lucifer, pale and shaken, finally found his voice. "I showed you this to make you acutely aware of our enemy's power. Despite our best efforts, God changed kingdoms in His own way, according to His schedule."

He leaned against the podium, as if exhausted, raising only his hand in a negative gesture to Nahash, who offered him a drink.

"God," Lucifer finally continued, "then influenced King Cyrus to make Daniel his prime minister and president of the royal cabinet of princes. To have Joseph become premier of Egypt was a damnable choice of heaven. To flaunt Moses as the adopted son of the pharaoh and later to see him overpower our people in Egypt was an even grosser indignity. But then to have Daniel, a Hebrew captive, become prime minister of two successive world powers is unforgivable!" Lucifer's fist slammed the podium in frustration.

Now he spoke slowly, with exaggerated articulation. "Listen carefully to me. A portion of the Cyrus prophecy remained unfulfilled. Isaiah predicted that the general would order the rebuilding of Jerusalem. Your finest team was provided to prevent this. Yet, Cyrus not only allowed the return of every willing Jew but he sanctioned it from our throne!"

"Your orders were absolutely clear," observed Ariun, "but even you have admitted that our efforts with these prophecies have been useless."

Lucifer jerked, as though feeling the sting of a fresh wound. Yet he did not seem to skip a beat.

"I suppose your hosts have done their best, but our best is still far from good enough. Nearly 50,000 returned with those scoundrels, Zerubbabel and Joshua. And with them returned the vitality of their faith. Yet, our local servants were able to stop the building of the Temple by false accusations. The Jews were so discouraged that victory again seemed within our reach. Who was it that was supposed to be guarding against any more prophets stepping in? We had them in the palms of our hand until Haggai and Zechariah arrived! The Temple would still be undone if your lines of defense had been ready.

"Then there is the matter of King Ahasuerus and Queen Esther. Haman was our top man—destined for the throne and for the destruction of every Jew on the face of earth. He was so perfectly taught and so like us. Everything was set, the plan was in full motion, and we let it slip through our hands. Who was it that was supposed to watch out for Mordecai? One old man, a nobody, a nothing—orders were to destroy him. And why was it that one young woman could not be corrupted with the riches of our throne or at least be driven with fear for her fate. You underestimate the power of the enemy."

"You have long made this clear," Ariun persisted, "but some of us would like to hear your specific design!"

Yet Lucifer ignored him.

Indignation began to swell among the ranks of even the loyal as they were blamed for Lucifer's woes. They knew full well they were not in charge of the operations. They knew that the Master was venting personal frustration. And they knew that more was coming.

"It amazes me as well that when Artaxerxes came to the throne after our disaster with Esther, that you would allow both Ezra and Nehemiah to find their way into the king's court! Were our hosts there too beaten to resist these enemy spies?

You allowed Ezra to return to Jerusalem with both willing Jews and our own finances. No doubt it's time to rearrange the placing of some of our troops and commanders. Ezra was carrying back the most destructive weapon against us—the teaching of the Law to the ordinary dwellers around Jerusalem—and you all knew it! Reestablishing the Temple worship was one thing, but the clear teaching of God's Word! He has torn to shreds the efforts of our workers around Jerusalem.

"You bungled affairs with Nehemiah. First, you were to have prevented him from finding a position in the court. Second, you failed to poison his soul in an environment totally dictated by our leading officers. Third, you should have been able to convince the king that Nehemiah was far too essential for the running of affairs in the court to be allowed to return to Jerusalem. And fourth, you allowed the king to make him an official of the Persian Empire, appointing him as governor of Judah. You allowed a man stirred by the Father to counter your best moves and rebuild the walls of Jerusalem. That was the final blow and the final outrage!"

"We have had enough of this . . ." Rasha growled to Raa. Even the most loyal of Lucifer's commanders were by now roasting in anger and Lucifer could see that his rehashing of past failures was inviting anarchy. In his typical form, he quickly switched topics to cool down tempers.

"God has overruled our use of the Persian kings to get the Jews back into the land from which we drove them. The Temple worship is in full swing, the Law is again on the center stage, and the people have enjoyed a time of relative peace and prosperity. Such have been their victories.

"We still have the vast majority of the Jews spread in captivity throughout our empire. Some of them have been successfully converted to our style of worship, but others have shown a tenacity to the Law that has amazed even me."

Rasha had taken as much of the lecturing as he could handle and stood to interrupt. "You once used the Egyptians," he interrupted Lucifer, "to torment God's people by making them do their work without straw. It was a delightful method for those we hate, but why are you tormenting us with the same device? We are well aware of the problems we now face and even more aware that our methods have not been working with these troublemakers. As a whole, they seem to have lost their love for worshiping our host of gods and goddesses. It's as though they have deeply learned something through this period of captivity. Perhaps it's time to change our method rather than rearrange our personnel?"

Lucifer smiled as if Rasha's wisdom had turned a light on the darkened matter. "Yes . . . yes . . . that's exactly what needs to be done. We have perhaps exploited our use of idolatry upon these people to the maximum. Our alternative would be to move them in the other direction—a direction that few of their people have ever walked in. Ezra and Nehemiah have utterly convinced the people that their promise of remaining in the land and under God's blessing rests upon their obedience to the Law. If it's Law they want, we can give them Law. More Law than they ever dreamed possible. We will make them legalists like God has never seen!"

Now Rasha was nodding as he smiled.

"This is our new program for destruction and confusion," Lucifer continued. "Make sure that we develop it gradually. Create issues: What is considered work on the Sabbath? When should one wash his hands to be ceremonially pure? We will build and build until the laws are complete beyond any man's comprehension. Make them appear as God's handiwork. Once convinced that the Father has spoken these laws, we have them in our hands and the Word will have lost its power against us. We shall create enmity and theological confusion that will defeat the Messiah."

The demons now were sitting forward in their seats. Here, they seemed to agree, was a workable plan.

"Let us work then to set up the grandest religious confusion and bitterness on earth. These people love to argue and reason. They will serve our purposes well. Create as many distortions as possible among them, especially regarding notions of the Messiah. When He comes, we will be waiting for Him. By then, no one will even recognize Him. His life will so contradict the legalism and false notions we have used that He will be hated by the most revered religious leaders among God's people. Hate breeds murder, you know. And it will be death for Him!"

New fires were now glowing in the eyes of all in leadership. This indeed was a plan with a future.

"And finally today," Lucifer hissed, "our most satanic and promising device now is our use of magic, the occult, astrology—any spiritualistic tool. We will resort more to subtle counterattack and clever counterfeit than frontal attack. Your work with the pagans has given me great satisfaction in captivating them with mysticism and conversations with the dead."

There was sporadic applause, less out of certainty than hope.

"Yours is a most diabolical work of deception, yet you cannot allow yourselves to be deceived! Some of you are yet novices in the arts of distortion, forgeries, and impersonation of God and of the dead. I will personally visit your nether regions and teach these exotic skills. For example, we will promote reincarnation to weaken men's belief in judgment and bodily resurrection."

Lucifer hesitated, hoping that a pause might deepen impression. But Ariun, the "cunning one," interpreted the delay as mere hesitation and quickly asked, "You say we will use reincarnation to weaken faith?"

"You heard me well," retorted the Master.

"But," returned Ariun, "this seems to be a contradiction."

"Remember first, young devil," Lucifer answered superciliously, "most of mankind need not consciously join us. It is enough that individuals do not consistently commit their way to God. Interrupt their daily worship routine. Without frequent contact with God, they will rely on man. Such self-directed persons are effective soldiers for us. They help guarantee our victory.

"Get others to hate us. Keep them so busy hating that they lose sight of the Father's power and love for them—which we cannot hope to match. Our only prospect of winning is to defeat the messages of the Godhead.

"Blind man to the certainty that effect follows cause. As I told you centuries ago, induce him to forget that God alone is able to give life. Insure that man is unaware he chooses eternal death by separating himself from the Source of life; blind him to the fact that God destroys no man.

"I remind you further that it is necessary to disguise yourself as harmless sheep. Some of you are much too impetuous, too eager to consume your prey at once. So some bright people, even youngsters like Abel and Joseph and David and Josiah and, yes, Daniel, have made you look like fools. Touch the conscience most tenderly at first. Anaesthetize it before you burn or cut. Then sear it with utmost caution, adapting your skills to the many facets of each personality and mind."

Lucifer smiled and winked, his spirits rising. "Devil possession will increasingly become one of our most satanic techniques. Remember how it performed magic for us in the courts of the Medes? We will set up task forces and name them by their goals—lust, sex, alcohol, drugs, depression, laziness, gossip, accusation, gluttony, and a thousand more.

"It is our business to tease, to deceive, and to bring people to death. Substitute peer dependency and social pressures for self-worth. There is no depth of deceit like that of the one who deceives himself, no arrogance like that of the man who ignores God. And there is no destruction like the eternal death we bring. Whether a person is active or passive in his iniquity, if we can divert him from complete allegiance to his Maker, we have all of him.

"I expect to come much closer to you in the ages ahead. We are reorganizing for our most powerful and diabolical effort as we anticipate the coming of the Messiah. You are my very surrogates in each personal conflict with man."

Turning to Ariun and Rasha, Lucifer glowed with an angry excitement. "We have lost some battles, but we will win the war!"

The demon horde arose as one to applaud their Master.

14
THE GRECIAN SYNDROME

The picture opened with less agitation than the last. "I am greatly relieved tonight," Lucifer began, "that Daniel and Esther, Ezra and Nehemiah, our godly tormentors, are far behind us, and that Israel is almost dead."

The assembly laughed, but Lucifer remained sober.

"You are making a good beginning with the occult. Keep it up! We will spend much time on that in future sessions, but," Lucifer said, tapping the podium with the knuckle of his first finger, "tonight I speak of Greece.

"Young Alexander from Macedonia was magnificent in conquering the Persian empire. Though he represented the fulfillment of Daniel's prophecy, he also has been highly useful to us. We have spread the Greek culture throughout the civilized world with one swift stroke of his hand. We have taught him deeply in the ideals of Homer's "Iliad" and of Aristotle's genius. We may not have been able to stop what God had planned, but we have had little trouble in distorting them.

"The spirit and zeal of Alexander to spread the Greek culture everywhere was effectively passed along to each of the prophesied divisions of his empire. Thanks to your colossal efforts a new tide of disorientation has swept over the world. Wherever the Greeks have gone they have taken both their mythology and philosophy. We will make these the center of education—the learning of the elite—to the end of time. Watch what that does to the centrality of the Scriptures!"

The demons applauded.

"We will thoroughly corrupt Greek culture. We will 'hellenize' the world to its very end."

"Hear, Hear," the devils shouted.

"We have made steady progress in saturating the Law-lovers with a double-dose of legalism. Those of you involved with that project are to be congratulated. You have been very careful to not overdose them!

"A few incidents have perplexed me though. It has happened so many times that I almost expect it. Why was it when Alexander swept south through Tyre and Gaza that you did not have him destroy Jerusalem as he had destroyed other cities. The city was to have been levelled! Yet you let them get away again! In training Alexander, why was he left to give heed to dreams? God again stepped in and saved the city of blasphemy.

"But . . ." Raa tried to get in a word of defense.

Lucifer deliberately turned from him, but immediately shifted his approach.

"You were successful," he soothed, "in getting him to take along a good number of Jews to Alexandria. Alexandria has become a center for our demoralizing of the Greeks. We will surely contaminate every resident of the city. Thanks also to some of your nether efforts Jews have emigrated wholesale to Antioch and our most enticing pleasures. I expect to reap a great crop from these works.

"I am having some second thoughts, though, about one of our projects in Alexandria. We all agreed that it would be a powerful blow to God's Word to have the Greek-speaking Jews translate the Hebrew Scriptures into Greek. Some of you convinced me that through this we could more effectively 'hellenize' the renegades and also corrupt God's Word. You found Ptolemy II to be a willing proponent of the project and it was done so smoothly. Did any of you wonder at the time that it might have gone all *too* smoothly? It has so haunted me these years that I am calling an alert to make sure that this project reaches our goals.

"But I wonder if we haven't pushed too hard in 'hellenizing' the Jews. I am afraid that Antiochus IV has gone too far. No one was more delighted than I with his destruction of much of Jerusalem and the setting up of the cult worship of Zeus in the Temple. I too laughed with delight when the herd of swine were driven through the Temple and the swine's flesh was offered on the altar. And the swine broth being sprinkled on the Holy of Holies—I've waited centuries for such revelry! Filling the courts with orgies and Antiochus' utter commitment to destroy every form of Jewish religion reminds me of our heart's desire, and for that spirit I am glad.

"But a reaction has set in! A wave of godly heroism has sprung up that was not expected. Look out for this fellow, an old man as a matter of fact, Mattathias by name. Your intelligence information handed out before this lecture describes the Maccabeans thoroughly. Don't be caught off guard by them!

"The Greeks have been a people who were easy to use. The vast success you have enjoyed over them, while commendable, should not be misunderstood. Any people who swell with pride in intellectual attainments, philosophy, and debate, are our easiest of targets. You have done well but it is time to redouble our efforts. The Messiah is coming and the world must be totally prepared to pervert Him! All of the reforms we have instituted have been nesting places for otherwise unlikely moral changes, which I believe we can use to cloak a vast array of perversions.

"The Greeks have been particularly vulnerable to your sexual devices and are ready for more changes. Both Alexandria and Antioch, our great Grecian metropolises, are overflowing with immorality. Let every center become a pioneering station that infiltrates every city."

Suddenly Lucifer became rigid and flushed. He obviously was trying to control a fierce anger. Yet he spoke slowly.

"We tempted Alexander to make Babylon the capital of his empire and he listened carefully. But he is dead. And we have not influenced *even one* of his successors to adopt this plan. Instead, they have used Babylon's bricks to build their palaces and dams on the Tigris River. And," he spat out, "all that now dwell in our city are wild beasts, ostriches, dancing satyrs and ... some of you! This humiliation shall not continue."

"But," reminded Rasha boldly, "our demons live there because of your command."

Lucifer was momentarily stunned. "So be it," he finally muttered. "Let it be the beginning, not the end."

Raa now joined Rasha in the challenge. "Just exactly how do you expect us to proceed? We enjoy these recriminations even less than you."

For the moment Lucifer was trapped by his own thoughtless words. These were his top generals. They obviously were not stupid. And more than that, he could not really do much to them; they were vital to his desperate campaign.

"Do not allow these Scripture prophecies to intimidate you," Lucifer now admonished, with little more than a nod at Rasha and Raa. "I tell you, we must distort their fulfillment—turn them to our own use."

"Master," interjected Moot, "we remind you again of how little we can control the Word of God."

Lucifer bent over the podium as if in agony, then spoke on as if nothing had happened.

"A case in point: Now that Alexander is dead, Greece is divided as prophesied, and, in theory, that can open the way for Israel's revival. But we will distract both the Greeks and the Jews in more devious ways.

"You are to use your most devious efforts to persuade people to become skeptical of the Messiah's promised redemption. Remember, as I told you before, to create expectations of His coming as an earthly king instead of the servant which Isaiah foretells so that when the Messiah does come they will not recognize Him."

The group laughed nervously. There was a long pause. Even the rash Raa seemed optimistic.

"This," Lucifer continued, "will lead to reform. And we must allow it to be so. Yet such reforms are possible nests for otherwise unlikely moral changes, which we can use to cloak a vast array of perversions.

"Greece is vulnerable to sexual devices, but you dare not be hasty or presumptuous. You are well aware of the unsuccessful efforts made to bribe Alexander with boy prostitutes. You forgot that he was a Macedonian and not a classically Hellenic intellectual. Yet you performed brilliantly in turning the affections of parents from their children, and children from their parents." Lucifer now was grinning.

"We have observed that conquering nations are those with strong family lines. This was even true with Alexander despite the lust-hungry nation we made of Greece. We will now decimate Greece by destroying its families.

"Abortion and child neglect will be logical outcomes of your devilish assaults on God-ordained marriage. Redouble your efforts to make adultery acceptable to all. This will help to dehumanize the treatment of children and debase marriage as a symbol of the relationship of God and His people. Concentrate also on perverting the sexual desires of males so that they enjoy cohabitation with one another as well as with women. You have done well in this, but your efforts have produced only a shadow of what must come.

"Our next logical step will be to make popular the use of boy prostitutes. National leaders can be defiled if provided with such boys as rewards for political favors. Remember also to bring your 'young temptations' to the generals of the army. Never mind that earlier leaders would not tolerate them. Those in power now are less interested in an integrated nation than in their own pleasure and power. Those watching the leaders will quickly follow their example. This is a further chance to make fidelity a joke and marriage a curse.

"These perverted relationships will deny God's purpose for the procreative act: the unity of sex and the oneness between mankind and God. No children can possibly issue from such liaisons, so the family—and human society—will be weakened."

Ariun looked at Gonev and over to Rasha and Raa. All were now pleased. This bold device would of course debase women. Such men would give little attention or love as worthy friends or mates. So women would be stirred to assert their own independence and demand their own license, even to relegate their children to slaves for the most casual of care, even to nurse at the breast.

"The time," said Lucifer, "has come for you to see that society no longer expects women to lead in upholding moral standards. Instead, lead them to demand the right to live their own lives, to do with their bodies as they please. Glamorize prostitutes as the admired playgirls of the nation's leaders, to be emulated by even the plainest little farm girls of the countryside."

The demons grinned.

"Go slowly, as always, yet as fast as it is possible to change culture and mores. Eventually people will be so tolerant of homosexuals, they will even appoint them as priests and as their spiritual leaders.

"Loose the bonds of marriage. Ridicule men who restrict their wives' or daughters' sexual activity. Multiply adultery and divorce. And cause women, like men, to crave sex with their own kind." It was clear from demon smiles that Lucifer was well heard.

"Again, the logical result will be the fragmentation of the family. The children will have no place to go, no one who really cares. We have already arranged that almost from birth they have been placed in the hands of surrogates or slaves. Now we will try to see that they receive less affection and care than the offspring of beasts. The day has come for child neglect, abortion, and infanticide on a national scale. This promises the most fruitful kind of violence and crime, for children will have no respect for their elders, and elders will receive what they deserve. As human values are diluted, the human spirit will ultimately be crushed, and patriotism and productivity will be destroyed. In their selfishness, people lose their sense of mutual responsibility and love for others.

"Declare that all of this is progress, and"—he grinned and rubbed his hands together—"they will be our people, our nation. The Grecian rule will collapse, and we will continue to poison other nations with even more potent venom until this 'serpent' wipes man from the face of the earth."

The audience burst into applause.

"This political and moral collapse will also turn their minds irrevocably from the God of heaven. Remember the Deity designed that fathers were to represent God to their young ones. The demonic behavior of their parents will make God hateful to such children. As atheists reject God, we will supply them gods of our own making, turning Jehovah into a useless myth."

Lucifer's face changed, hardened. His stern gaze fell on each officer; some squirmed under his stare as he began pacing before them. Yet others viewed him impassively, and he knew it.

"Before I leave you tonight, I am compelled to remind you again of the great crisis we face. As you well know, the demon or man who discounts the prophets is a fool." He stopped pacing and pounded the podium. "We make fools out of men, but we dare not fool ourselves. If we are to believe the prophecies, as we must, the Messiah will be coming soon.

"It is crucial that Israel continue more and more to look for the Messiah as a conquering king. Whether by distraction or deceit, ridicule, murder, or kingdoms destroyed, you must overlook no diversion or device which may abort His true mission. The Greeks' liberal arts and sciences—note the word 'liberal'—will increasingly replace the Word of God in education. They will laugh at the hunger for truth.

"On an international level, strengthen all efforts given to the spreading of Eastern cult worship. Men all over the world are becoming dissatisfied with our infiltration of the Greek's philosophy and mythology. As precise and refined as these are, they have not satisfied the deep cries of the human spirit. Men are still looking heavenward and the 'mystery' religions we have been developing for centuries should fill this void.

"We want to especially push those religions which include a theme of redemption and eternal life. Attis in Asia Minor, Osiris in Egypt, Mithras in Persia, and others will be well suited for our purposes. We need spokesmen—preachers—to carry these messages and refill the heads of men with strange and perplexing mysteries that cannot be verified but can only be experienced. Make the mystical and the transcendental appear to hold the promise of new life and deliverance. Be sure they have profound experiences that will be proclaimed in every community. The time has come to expand religious concepts in every field. When the Messiah comes, we must control every religious system!"

Lucifer now spoke slowly, in measured words. "The Son's success is our death decree. If we win, our satanic future is eternally confirmed. There must be no effort unspent nor any doubt that we shall overcome."

The demons filed out as their leader turned slowly away, deep in thought, attended only by Nabal and Raa.

15
CONFUSION CONCERNING THE MESSIAH

This scene showed the great hall packed with officers. They were in a mood of unusual anticipation. The word had gone out that Lucifer would announce some extraordinary plans. As usual, the angel demons stood as he entered, but a curt motion of his hand quickly commanded them to be seated.

"This meeting today may be the most important session in our history," he began solemnly. "With the possible exception of our planning time for Eden, this is *the* crucial convocation. First, your efforts to debase Greece were brilliant and fruitful as you carried out my mandates to the letter. You were exactly on target in elevating Plato above God as the source of truth. World morality has reached a new low.

"Now the powerful hordes of Rome, gaining their strength from primitive values couched in a family-centered society, have overrun Greece. I order you to repeat in Rome the same self-deception that weakened Greece. Bind them with threads of concern for themselves until they become a band of iron that closes them in." Lucifer's great hands came together, his fingers taut as they met in a fierce gripping gesture.

"The Romans have conquered above all others. The treasures of the nations have flowed into the hands of the wealthy in Rome. This must be fully developed. Your work has gone smoothly in the development of senseless luxury, debauchery, and corruption of the ruling classes. International banks and the large estates, slaves beyond imagination and the disintegration of the middle class, the idle poor crowding into bread lines—now is the time to upgrade our development of Caesar into the position of one to be worshiped.

"Let all nations look to him as the final authority on all matters regarding their lives. Establish the Imperial cult for his worship and make all those who refuse to submit to his worship be regarded as outlaws with no rights. Make it the test of the loyalty of the citizen. We shall use the power of Rome against the Messiah.

"Regarding Rome itself, as noted before, your efforts have them at our mercy. Divorce has become so rampant and unaccompanied by legal blame that all sense of guilt has been removed, except as it serves our darkest purposes. As in Greece, sexual immorality has destroyed the meaning of marriage vows and opened the floodgate to popularizing abortion and infanticide. Homemaking and parenthood have become such a drudgery that parents are responding to our social pressure and placing young children in the care of the state before their values are established. Cause this movement to snowball.

"See that narcissism moves into the female domain," he went on. "We project that self-centered drives will inevitably make the rich richer and the poor poorer, creating unrest, violence, and eventually rebellion. In the end the military will be unable to contain the uprisings, and Rome will, like Greece, be ripe for the taking by the barbarians around them.

"Convey hopes of riches without responsibility, of achievement without effort, and of heaven's blessings without obedience. Weave them through and through—peasant, peon and king—with the relaxation of their values.

"And the children—confuse them; throw their lives into disarray. Make them so dependent on their peers that they will lose all self-direction and freedom in their thinking. They will make excellent candidates for the Roman legions."

There was a murmur of approval.

"Proceed to prostitute Rome so that in historical perspective, it will be perceived as the most sordid and morally corrupt of all empires. Exhaust its vital forces until the aberrant tastes of its people create memories loathesome to future generations. This will insure divine retribution which we will use to demonstrate the sadism of God."

The demons grinned.

"We will make the iron nation into a carnal showcase!"

"You are now experienced in raping civilizations!" Lucifer looked at Laylah, the one called "night."

"We destroy families," Laylah called out.

The demon officers again nodded with satisfaction at this strategy.

"These," proclaimed Lucifer, "are our Roman plans for the next centuries. But I have more immediate concerns, as I am sure you have anticipated, for I find your minds to be closer to mine than ever before."

The demon throng smiled and even politely applauded. Lucifer's tone changed. His face held anger and surprise.

"The Messiah is with us!" He hissed. A wave of shock rolled through the assembly accompanied by gasps and in most cases trembling.

"I do not speak with pleasure. Lest some of you have doubts, I assure you that He is real. As promised in Scripture, He has come 'as a root out of dry ground.' There is nothing kingly about Him. His appearance would hardly raise an eye among the crowds. He has been working with His father in the family carpenter shop from the time He could talk and has been so busy with household chores that He has had little time to play. He is already twelve and has hardly left His hometown."

Lucifer's fists were knots of rage. He released his words one by one through clenched teeth.

"He is the single greatest threat to our kingdom," he shouted. "This is a matter of life and death—His, or yours and mine!

"The Son of God will assure His people that He came to tear away the exactions which we have led Israel to weave around His Law. Christ is determined to prove that His Law is a mirror of love. We have persuaded stupid man that the Law is a rock of hate, a cruel and impossible burden, and cannot possibly bring happiness and peace. God portrays it as a set of guidelines for their safety. We have made the Law into a wilderness of statutes.

"Following my instructions, you have become devilishly adept at portraying God as an unforgiving despot who watches with a shrewd and accusing eye to ferret out the people's mistakes. Man has increasingly come to view Him as an overbearing taskmaster and a sadistic Judge who delights in watching His victims writhe in hell. Yet if we allow the Messiah to fulfill His promises, He will dispel this concealing fog. So I am calling you to double duty to destroy the Messiah's mission."

Lucifer noticed Herev whispering to Ebed at his side.

"If you have something to say, tell us all," he admonished impatiently.

"I merely stated," replied the devil of the "sword," "that it will take more than double duty to meet your demands."

"We will watch your example, Herev," spat Lucifer.

"We have," he continued, "watched Christ's ancestors year by year and age by age in anticipation of His coming. Since the announcement of His conception in the womb of Mary, I have monitored His progress moment by moment. We did our best to kill Him, as a few of you are aware, and had the insane Herod destroy Bethlehem's male children. But an angel warned Joseph, and the family escaped." His eyebrows peaked, his eyes pierced his audience. "Hoshek," he called suddenly. "What are you doing with the Son's virgin birth?"

The "darkness" demon leaped up. "We will treat it as a deception rather than as a miracle of God," he said.

His master nodded. "Well said, Hoshek."

The dark one was delighted at Lucifer's verbal applause and added, "Throughout Nazareth we have spread the story that He is illegitimate and His mother of ill repute."

But Lucifer's smile passed. "We planned that the schoolboys and village rabble would contaminate the boy," he growled, "but we have been thwarted by His program of work with His parents at home. In fact, they seldom allow Him out of their sight."

"But," interrupted Ariun, "soon He will go to the Temple as is the annual custom of His people, and we could contrive to separate Him from His parents there."

"Excellent," Lucifer responded. "I will handle this personally. And as time moves on I will take charge of tempting Him. I will place Him under such sensuous coercion as no person has ever survived. He must be destroyed.

"I need make Him slip only once in a split-second thought or word or action—in anger or impatience or disrespect or lust—and He will sacrifice His mission. If we can cause Him to loosen his dependence upon the Father for one moment, we destroy Him."

Applause thundered, but Lucifer raised his hand.

"Save your energy," he directed, "for this greatest of all satanic efforts just ahead, since you are the stage workers for this drama of all ages. I must have your total, most insidious efforts. We must so warp every actor on our stage, every circumstance in the Messiah's life, that somehow, someday He will break His dependence upon the Father, thus proving it impossible—as we maintain—for man to live in accordance to God's so-called law of love.

"We worked for centuries to be totally prepared, and our lines of defense have never been stronger. Our work to divide the nation religiously has the people in a complete state of confusion. The Sadducees play into the hands of the Romans and control both the high priesthood and the Temple. They are so power-crazed that even the most simple of men can see they view religion as a means to wealth and security. The sinister blackness of their hearts knows no depth. And their hate for the Pharisees—this is a wall which can never be torn down.

"The Pharisees are so embroiled in our additions to the Law that they will fly in the face of the Son. They will never tolerate His pure love for the Father and His delight in service. The pride that divided them into schools of interpretations will be enflamed as a torch to continually torment the Son. They will be so inhuman in their demands upon man that the Son will rise to curse them. Already they regard the common Jew as a complete ignoramus.

"The Zealots will be anxious to use Him as their king and will gladly test his commitment to the Messianic promises of deliverance from the foreign yoke. Let all the work we have done on distortions concerning His role now bear their fruit!

"Herod Antipas is much like his father for corrupting and must be positioned to scorn the Son. And the Roman despot in charge of this territory—make sure we bring in one who is both heartless and a coward. We will need a man who fears Rome and is afraid to stand on his own conscience and reason. Look for a bully and yet a weakling. He must be found!

"You will work on Christ's family, especially His brothers. Fill them with innuendo, ridicule, impatience, and deceit. Devise overwhelming temptations through His home-life. Beat Him until He breaks down!

"We have accused God of being arbitrary in His demands upon us and all of His creatures." Lucifer grinned, yet his eyes were dark pools of hate. "This is our chance—our final chance—to prove to the universe that we are right and God unfair and unjust!"

He paused, looking across the vast assembly. Nervous laughter spattered the quiet, and Lucifer jerked around at the sound. His face flushed; his voice was harsh and stern.

"There is no time for levity! Your lives are at stake."

"And yours, also," reminded the bold Raa.

Momentarily stunned, Lucifer quickly admitted, "Yes, mine too."

"And everything you stand for," added Raa.

Lucifer was obviously irritated at his demon prince of evil, but nevertheless answered, "Indeed.

"If Jesus Christ survives," he continued, "or even dies without sin, our days are numbered. You are to follow the orders of your commanders with meticulous care. This is our only chance to destroy the Messiah as the incarnation of divinity on earth."

He looked across the throng and each servant felt his leader's eyes bore into his soul.

"Do you understand?" he screamed.

Replies of affirmation echoed throughout the vast assembly.

16
THE MESSIAH'S DISRUPTION

The nearly dark screen reflected the somber mood of the demon audience as this episode began. After a long and troubled delay, Lucifer took his place at the podium. The fallen angels gathered before him seemed to shrink from his piercing and worried gaze. His face was a mask of hatred, yet no subject could fully read his thoughts. He began slowly and heavily to speak.

"Our reckoning day has come . . . and it has gone. The enemy has won the decisive battle of the war."

He stopped, coughed. Then his voice grew stronger.

"But we will defy Him to the end. The Son of God has treated our kingdom of darkness as a common pawnshop. When the Deity laid down death as the penalty for sin, that had to be also the cost of redemption. And as I told you before, that price obviously had to be paid by the Creator who would somehow become a creature. Now the Son of God has done exactly that, and He has redeemed mankind from our grasp."

Lucifer's great fist made the podium shake.

"I tell you I will harass Him to my final breath. I am going to seize every candidate for His kingdom on whom I can lay my hands. And I guarantee you that no more than a remnant shall escape. And that remnant shall pay a heavy price!"

[I thought again of Gabriel's early reminder that the real Center of this story—the One on which our minds must dwell—was the Savior, the Example, who paid the price before us. Satan would now no longer have the credibility with his demons that his ego demanded.]

He stopped, making an effort to control himself. His voice came low, with a slow and deliberate delivery. "We are all in this together. We have no options; there is no return. Long ago we made our choice. But it is our diabolical privilege to take as many with us as we can. I assume, therefore, that all of you are with me in utter defiance of God."

He paused, his open hand held high over his head. "Is this true?" he shouted. "I want no half-hearted helpers. Are you with me in total defiance of our enemy?"

The crowd leaped to their feet, with shouts of "Hear, Hear," and thundering applause. Though jubilant they too appeared wounded in battle. Lucifer stood, arms outstretched, soaking up the adoration while his features seemed to merge from rage to pride, then finally to deep hatred. "I knew you would!" he called out, motioning them to be seated. His words came faster, frantically, like the hoofbeats of a runaway horse.

"We must tear the flock of the enemy to pieces!" he shrieked. "We are to fulfill the prophecies of Isaiah, Jeremiah, Ezekiel and Daniel with demonic fury. We will make God's pastors into dumb dogs who allow those around them to be devoured. We will goad unfaithful watchmen into our service and betray His trust, as they shepherd their flocks to hell."

Again applause swelled.

"And *I* applaud *you*!" He clapped his hands for the first time in their recollection. Then he spoke slowly and with great emphasis. "Nevertheless, I caution that you are dealing with powers who know your every thought. You must, more than ever, be wolves in sheep's clothing in order to deceive even the very elect of God.

"And now, a brief review of the past twenty years. Give these principles and methods your closest attention and support, remembering well these facts.

"At age twelve the Christ Child went to the Temple in Jerusalem, and we did succeed in separating Him from His parents. Yet, He did not leave the Temple to relax with the indolent masses or peep with the other boys at the houses of ill fame." Lucifer shook his head, still disbelieving. "His will seemed fixed. He was resolute. Angels guarded Him."

Something like a sigh escaped Lucifer's lips.

"We dare not ignore the scriptural promises that *any* servant of God may have this angelic protection," he cautioned. "Our only hope is to get to the children as early as possible. Plague them with the habits of their wine-bibbing and narcotic-drunk parents. Lead them to expect and demand more than life can ever give them. You did well, leading Israel to expect a king and turning the people from a carpenter's son. And you did a devilish job of harassing the Christ in His own home, using His brothers to heap ridicule upon Him and belittle His work. But learn a lesson from this, my colleagues: In the end, Christ's example was so strong that He influenced even His brothers to follow them.

"Then God filled Christ's baptism with threatening symbolism. Observe that John baptized Him in the Jordan River to symbolize the burial of sin. He clearly performed as a model, for"—Lucifer gagged on the words—"for He lived without sin."

The Adversary pointed at Lashan. "What are Christ's followers claiming about this? What do they claim baptism means to their believers?"

Lashan looked around uneasily. In that moment revulsion washed over him as he relived Christ's baptism and recalled the joy on His face.

Lucifer impatiently jerked his head at his "slave," and Lashan spoke quickly. "They claim that in baptism a believer shows he has been washed of sin and"—his voice faltered—"has risen to a new life."

Lucifer's face purpled. "I command you to destroy this symbolic act. I don't care how you handle it—by deceit, diversion, substitution or elimination. I require only that you totally spoil its significance for the emerging Christian Church. And don't forget that in our gospel the dove that came to Christ at His baptism was not the Holy Spirit, but our pagan goddess, Semiramis—the third person of our satanic trinity. Teach that!"

Lucifer seemed spent, drained, beaten. Clearing his throat,

he started to speak, then stopped, obviously having difficulty in organizing his thoughts. His servants shifted nervously, uneasily, and a low murmur rippled across the ocean of puzzled faces. Not even after the flood had they seen their leader like this. At last he regained a measure of composure.

"Again I must warn you of the changes that have taken place in those chosen of Christ, the ones they call disciples," he said, retrieving his thoughts. "Among these were uncouth fishermen, and taxgatherers, despised even by their own people." He began pacing.

"Now look at them! They are articulate spokesmen for the Messiah, brilliant in their witness and fearless of opposition. Don't forget to move among them as wisely and silently as the serpents you are, using every possible device to trap them in criticism and conflict.

"The record of miracles by the Son of God is a terror to us," Lucifer went on. "And driving you out of so many of our possessions was effortless for Him. But let us learn today of His greatest weapon which He used on me. It was His use of the Word of God to bring me to His feet, when He should have bowed at mine!"

There was a long silence; heads were bent low. Each demon remembered the starved, weakened Christ after forty days of wilderness fasting.

"I warn you urgently and insistently that the Scriptures can serve His followers in the same way they served Him. You will do well to better understand God's written Word, for it is one of the most despised weapons of terror they have against us. This sword must be dulled until its cutting edge is gone and can no longer do us damage.

"I adjure you! Carefully study Christ's use of God's Word. If you don't master it, it will master you!"

Lucifer's fist slammed into the podium. "Our top priority is to guard from our subjects the secret of scriptural power."

Disbelief darkened his features. "Christ actually delighted to do the Father's will!"

His eyes were now narrow slits, his voice edged with hysteria. "I don't care how you do it—whether you drive them to kill their grandmothers or simply distract them from prayer—but you must seek to destroy their personal experience with *Him*." Lucifer spit out the word "Him" as if it were obscene.

"When they open their Bibles, when they kneel to pray, when their foolish minds turn to the Father, buzz around their thoughts like a gnat."

He leaned heavily on the podium—exhausted, yet determined to continue. The demon throng before him, seeing his haggard face and ashen skin, looked away. They, too, were angry and, far more terrible, frightened. Few had believed that the Son would degrade himself by living on earth as one of earth's children. When He left heaven and actually became a child of Mary, they were astounded. As He grew, matured and finally died—without sin—to save mankind, they knew unspeakable terror.

After a long pause, their leader spoke again.

"Of all the Christian gospel there is a no more loathsome fable than the grace of Christ. Get deep into your minds this declaration of Christ: the moment the sinner turns to Him in repentance and faith, Christ covers him with His own righteousness so that the sinner appears before heaven as perfect, cleansed from sin by Christ. This primary thought of the gospel must be destroyed.

"Remember that man's natural disposition is to be like us, for we controlled him. So we must keep him from accepting the salvation provided through Christ. You must do anything that will stress, disturb, confuse or destroy any communion between man and God. Make him deny the repurchasing power of the blood of Christ, insisting instead that he can save himself by his own efforts. Blind him to his need of a Savior so he chooses to reject Him.

"Some will accept God's saving grace. Therefore, teach them that once they surrender to God, they can live any way they want. Lead other teachers to proclaim that once people are saved they cannot sin anymore. You will make the child of God into a betrayer, and he will not even know it."

Lucifer laughed without joy. "We will laugh," he jeered, "in the face of God." He waited, needing to hear the applause.

"And that brings me to the cross. Despite every agency of deceit and every load of ridicule, I was not able to touch the Son of God with a single aberrant thought. In fact, I was thwarted even in His death. We were set to kill Him, but He actually gave up His life. Our only recourse now is to scar His memory and desecrate the cross. We will lead people into turning the celebration of Christ's birth into a pagan revel—a day of festivity more than of worship, of getting more than of giving, and of myths and tales and fading memories about the birth of Christ. See that this birthday is celebrated for me.

"We have yet another monumental base for our plans to bewilder and misdirect Israel—the new Christian Church—and all others who even remotely embrace the Scriptures as their guide. Undoubtedly some of you were as startled as I, that at the *moment* of Christ's death, when He commended His Spirit to His Father, the great heavy curtain which separated the holy place from the place of the Most Holy in the Temple was torn in two from top to bottom."

Lucifer raised high the fingers of both hands as if in a great tearing maneuver.

"This had to be done by an angel, or even the hand of God himself, for the curtain was heavier than a Persian carpet and too high for any high priest himself to reach. God's message was obvious: The historic Hebrew sacrificial system which pointed forward to the death of the 'Lamb of God' was finished.

"Now we must distort the communion service which Christ committed to the disciples and turn it into a substitute for the sacrificial system. Instead of reminding Christians of their Lord's death and its meaning, we will turn it into a ritual of works. We must corrupt the church so it perceives itself as the agent of salvation and teach that clergy take the place of Christ as their mediator with God. We will contrive for them a God of anger, impatience and retribution. And they will believe us—and fear."

"But," interrupted Rasha, who could no longer contain his resentment, "what do you have to tell us about the resurrection?"

A gasp went up from the assemblage, as Rasha struck a raw,

throbbing nerve of memory. Awe, astonishment, unspeakable terror—these emotions again flooded their minds.

"We of course had the tomb massively guarded," their leader continued, trying to retrieve his composure—and their confidence. "But we could not stop the angel of God nor the earthquake he stirred."

Sweat glistened on his face; he began to hyperventilate but fought for control. The throng before him mirrored his distress. They recalled themselves huddled around Christ's grave with the soldiers posted by Pilate. Some unconsciously covered their eyes, as they relived the moment of supreme horror when one angel, brilliant from the reflected glory of God, came to call forth Christ from the grave, and the Roman guard fell unconscious before him. The demon host and their fearless leader had been impotent before the power of a single representative of God.

Lucifer began to pace. He mopped his face and strode back and forth across the stage.

"But," he finally and boldly declared, "we will turn our defeat into an embarrassment for the Deity by linking Christ's resurrection to the pagan goddesses of fertility and liken it to the fecundity of the rabbit, and to the chicken and the egg. We will suggest the reemergence of life from the earth rather than from heaven, pointing to the day of the resurrection as the day of the sun. The sun and moon gods will be the gods of all gods, even as we have already installed their altar in the temple to all gods, the Pantheon of Rome!"

His pacing stopped. Lucifer leaned heavily on the podium. "We will portray Christ to the ages in a thousand diverse ways. We will use music, poetry, literature, theology and art to project Him variously as effeminate, extreme, homosexual, a lover of dissolute women—anything but a powerful, virile leader of men, and a shepherd to children. He said that people would become like Him when they see Him as He is—high and lifted up, a loving Savior."

He laughed in derision.

"Let us provide them a million saviors. I will appear as an angel of light and perform miracles before their eyes."

He stopped, his sharp senses detecting a ripple of surprise among Rasha and Raa and others of his staff.

"And why not?" he demanded. "Am I not the master of deceit! I can give disease and withdraw it. I can perform a million spiritualistic miracles. Millions will acknowledge me to be the very Christ."

Heads nodded, grins began to form.

"As I told you before, I plan to so use His professed servants that this game will deceive everyone that does not personally and intimately know Christ and His Word.

"I adjure you now to join me not only in diverting men from *principles* of the Word, but also in flaunting the directions of God. See that they think they are learning, but never let them actually come to a knowledge of the truth. Then," he added, his palm slamming the podium, "we will teach God a lesson. Separated from God, many will die!"

17
THE ROMAN SURROGATE

The film opened brightly, in sharp contrast to the last episode. Lucifer strode into the committee room, fist held high in triumph. Though he had never fully recovered from his encounter with Christ, outwardly he appeared in all his former glory. His select officials gave him polite applause.

"I hail you today as the overmastering disruptive force of the universe! These past centuries have seen wave after wave of attack upon the Christian Church, both from without and from within. Now with the coming of Constantine as the emperor, we have gathered to introduce a dramatic change in our designs for the servants of the enemy."

All the officers nodded their obvious satisfaction and to many it came as an extreme relief. The tactics employed in the past centuries (though inhumanely delightful) had proved less than spectacular in results. And as usual, when results were meager, blame was heavy.

"You are well aware that our primary weapon has been the persecution of believers by the Roman emperors. Early on your performance with the cruel Caligula and the derelict Claudius sparkled with genius, and the way you manipulated Nero to accuse the Christians of starting Rome on fire was brilliant indeed. The wave of murder and hate, and especially your handling of Paul and Peter, were diabolically clever. They had pummelled our kingdom almost beyond repair and their deaths were a good riddance."

Raa and Rasha were instrumental in this project and were joined by their colleagues in open grins.

"Our centuries of working to establish idol worship was so successful that it became interwoven into every phase of life. The Christians' refusal to take part in our civic ceremonies and festivals for the gods made them appear as anti-social, morose, and haters of other men. Then their refusal to worship the emperor made them appear disloyal and as revolutionaries.

"Nero and Domitian's rage in frenzy and hate drove them into secret meetings which aroused suspicion. Meeting before sunrise or late at night, often in caves or catacombs underground, it was easy to spread false reports about them. Rumors of lasciviousness and even of murderous, bloodly sacrifices made them the scourge of mankind. When we raised the shout, 'the Christians to the lions,' it was almost too easy to find a willing mob!

"Then we stirred up Marcus Aurelius who delighted in such destruction. Of the thousands of believers he had beheaded or devoured, Polycarp and Justin Martyr were my favorites. The wretch Polycarp, bishop of Smyrna, when commanded to curse Christ, answered, 'Eighty and six years have I served him and he has done me nothing but good; and how could I curse him, my Lord and Savior!' What a joy to burn such a dog alive! People thought twice before confessing Christ after that."

A restrained applause broke forth, but few meant it. Most of the commanders, though delighted to destroy any believer in the cruelest way possible, greatly feared the likes of Polycarp and were terrified of confessions like his.

"I have noticed," Lucifer continued, looking intently around at his audience, "that some of you are affected by the reactions of earth's children toward you. Never mind that these people are indifferent or even hate you. Don't be offended! Rather *encourage* the church to joke about you, to play games about you—anything to induce them to take you lightly. Be glad if they curse you, exult if they ridicule you, and be thrilled when they become so accustomed to you they are not persuaded that you really exist. Never fear, we will repay them and their God in our own way. We will desecrate His entire Law, making it so rigidly impossible to obey that man will turn from it in disgust. Now we will create less suspicion about our strategies if we convince people that His Law is a barrier to love and prosperity rather than the fruit of God's affection. Men must see the decalogue as a set of arbitrary rules instead of principles of love to guard and guide them." He made as if to spit on the floor. "The only law we know is the law of self . . . and death; the Golden Rule is valuable only when it is expedient."

"Please explain," interrupted Rasha, "just how we destroy God's Law."

Lucifer grinned. "We continue to make it a farce—from God's commands to honor Him and protect His name to His demands for moral purity and respect for life. You have adroitly shredded the fifth commandment—in taking natural affection of children away from parents and parents from children. I was particularly pleased with the bestial ways you taught the Greeks and Romans to get rid of their old people. Except for the Julian laws of Augustus, you have an almost complete record of depravity. When we persuade men to dishonor their parents," Lucifer raised his eyebrows, "we force them to disobey and dishonor their God.

"But you must also do much more in perverting God's command not to kill. Tell them that the Deity only prohibits murder. Teach them to be casual about suicide and abortion, and particularly about indifference to their own bodies—their food and drink and exercise and rest. Make them irregular in their habits, obscure the body as the temple of the Holy Spirit, and you waste them by their own choice. Let them view alcohol and drugs as physical and psychological remedies and recreation more than as harbingers of dementia and death. Let them kill themselves by their own dereliction and slay their brothers in their own hate-filled thoughts. Let them flaunt the Law in their stupidity.

"And the famous seventh commandment has been your savory game! You have made literal brothels of Greece and Rome," he smiled, nodding to Ebed. "You and your lieutenants have transformed earth's leading intellectuals into perverted and lecherous wretches. Do not stop until you make adultery and fornication—by thought and word as well as by act—acceptable recreation for all. Remember that when you prostitute the marriage relationship, you demonically distort the imagery of God with His church. Make it impossible for people to sustain relationships. That's what our game is all about," he chuckled, "to divide them, to separate them from each other and from God.

"Out attack on the eighth law also must be greatly broadened," he went on. "We will teach man to steal his neighbor's cattle or chariot or slave; show him how to burglarize a treasury, a museum, a home or even a grave; bring him into the art of counterfeit; see that he learns the skill of forgery and fraud; show even believers how to steal the affections of a wife from her husband and a husband from his wife. And ultimately you will succeed in turning their affection from God.

"And we laugh with delight at the ninth commandment."

A few officers laughed loudly with him. But Ebed and Gonev winced.

"The very nature of our satanic work is to turn the truth. You have performed admirably in the art of betrayal, but now more than ever we must make man an accuser of his brethren, his neighbor, and ultimately his God, even by silence or inaction when those methods serve us best.

"And don't forget the tenth commandment. Encourage people's hunger for anything that belongs to others—money, home, cattle, servants, or another's mate. They need not even understand their own motives, and often they will not—until they cannot stop themselves.

"I have only briefly outlined our line of assault on the decalogue," he went on. "We will see that Constantine and his successors use the iron power of Rome to revise heaven's decadent legal system. Through this ruse we will unify his declining empire."

There was a long pause. Then Lucifer shifted his train of thought.

"Yet, don't forget the Messiah died, without sin, though we maligned, taunted and ridiculed. We harassed and tortured Him—even to His death."

"But He lives again!" muttered Ebed, as Gonev nodded morosely.

Lucifer's "yes" told anger and futility. But he went on.

"We have embarrassed God and profaned His Law—which of course He holds before the universe as His own testament, the imprint of His character. But we have much farther to go in discrediting the Holy Spirit, proving Him a sham before Christians, pagans, and Jews. Man cannot understand the all-pervasive idea of omnipresence, which is a characteristic of the God-head. Yet His very cogency as the "Comforter" sent by Christ is dependent on His being received as the Holy *Spirit*.

"So we will rob Him of His personality. As we contrive to make people think of Him as a ghost, indistinguishable to most from the historic spirits of the gods which we have so cleverly used to haunt primitive pagans, we will make Him blend perfectly into our spiritualistic goals—as a purveyor of sorcery, magic and devilish apparitions."

"But with His power," protested Ebed, "that will be difficult."

Lucifer ignored his slavery demon. "We will confuse Christians by representing Him as One who will adapt to any and all church doctrines, conforming to their every religious whim. We will suggest that people can feel instant spiritual maturity, requiring no personal sacrifice, no consecration, and no ongoing surrender. Avoid all mention of His still small voice and obscure attention to Him as a quiet, powerful worker who gradually brings Christian maturity only with believers' continual yielding to the will of God."

Rasha and Raa frowned with Ebed, but Lucifer continued.

"Meanwhile, redouble your satanic work against the Roman family. You have already excelled in destroying the Julian laws. Continue now to shift sex roles, instill a hunger for luxury, and bring in more slaves to care for the children. It will not be difficult," he winked at Gonev, "for you to reduce traditional Roman industriousness."

Gonev eagerly agreed. "As you say," he grinned.

"With their increased leisure, satisfy their natural quest for entertainment with every possible kind of sport or amusement, including sexual excursion out of marriage. Thus we will slow the Roman birthrate, proliferate adultery, spread prostitution, increase abortion, diminish productivity and kill patriotism. As in the other cultures we have destroyed, induce the leaders and the rich to set the pace; the lesser folk will follow."

His finger tapped the desk. "You have ingeniously distorted the relationship of the descendants of Isaac and Ishmael, and we will deepen and expand this guilt. However, I now want you to develop hostilities against the Jews by the Christians. This will cut directly across God's ideal of love for all earth's children, as Christians conceive of a holy hatred against the Jews," he laughed, "and never imagine that it is from *us*, not God. And the Gentiles—ah, the presumption of their thinking that God will save only them."

He turned to Skahor. "A good project for your division," he commanded.

Skahor straightened, giving a curt nod. "I understand."

"Base your entire strategy on the demand of the Jewish leaders for Christ's death. And the writings of Eusebius and Tertullian remind me that we must stir within Christians a dependence on rituals—candles, holy water, images and vestments. We must divorce the Old Testament record from the New and destroy the integrity of the Scriptures which God is preparing. Focus men's minds on minute details so that they will look at words instead of principles and miss the larger message.

"Never forget that God designs to spread His gospel through believers. He tells them this sharing is a training program for eternity. We will prove this design is folly by preoccupying men so deeply with revelries and cares that they will have little time for any such gospel.

"But I caution you again to use great wisdom," he went on, his eyes swiftly moving from one demon face to the other. "Your feeble attempts to counterfeit the miracles of Paul in casting out demons is a case in point. In using the sons of Sceva you actually glorified Christ more than you honored me."

Heads dropped, eyes looked at the floor, except for Rasha and Raa.

"But," interrupted Rasha, "we are doing exactly as you directed."

"Circumstances change," shot back Lucifer, and continued without a further nod to his "devil of wickedness."

"Be careful of the direction your work takes. Be angry, even fierce in your work, but remember your greater rage is toward God. Hate Him with all the strength and ferocity in your being, but don't let your contempt for men override the way you handle them. Be guided, rather, by your superior satanic knowledge and power. As you did with Job, oppress every one, and wherever possible deepen oppression with depression until you ultimately possess them. And we will get the godly so busy working for God that they forget Him."

The demons grinned and nodded knowingly.

18
THE DARKEST OF THE AGES

[My angel host turned away momentarily from the screen. "The centuries after Christ were not easy for the fledgling Christian Church," Gabriel told me. "As you know from his lectures, after he was defeated, Lucifer redoubled his efforts against God. Destined to die, he determined to carry with him the majority of earth's children.

"He worked vigorously to see that the growing church became more concerned with survival and political power than with representing their Master. They became steeped in superstition and ignorance. And yet," he brightened, "God saw them as He sees all—individually. He loves each one of you as if you were the only person on the earth. And while we in heaven continue to celebrate Christ's victory, we also know unbounded joy with each person who submits his life to God through faith in the Savior. And," he went on, "like at all times, in the young church there always remained believers who were links between earth and heaven that Lucifer could not break! Although fully aware of Satan, they never dwelled on him. They were fully surrendered to Christ."

Now we turned to watch Lucifer again.]

The throng rose with applause for their leader. He strode back and forth across the stage until the ovation faded. No one could recall a longer ovation than this one.

"I am honored tonight as always by your sacrificial loyalty and selfless devotion," he began, tentatively clearing his throat.

He paused, and then started over again. "Once again we gather to review our past and our future. Thanks to your renewed and unceasing vigor you have fulfilled the prophecies, making darkness cover the earth and gross darkness the people. You have ushered in the darkest age—mentally, physically, and spiritually—that the world has ever seen!"

The crowd arose with one accord to bask in a seldom-given word of appreciation. All the pride and independence of the Fall seemed to rise from deep within them. Lucifer waited as the demon host applauded each other and then went on. "All of the programs instituted with Constantine have reaped an incredible harvest. Our most outstanding success has been the development of the papal authority. From the claim to be the head of the whole church we have moved him to a position claiming to rule over the nations as well, above kings and emperors. I wonder what Peter thinks about our using his name?"

Whistles and catcalls accompanied the drone of cheering and laughing of the host. The Apostle Peter had been a "rock" against them and many felt the delight of finally getting even.

"Pope Gregory I, 'the Great,' though extending the realm of the church in the conversion of the nations of Europe, paved the way for temporal power by making the church the virtual ruler of the province around Rome. His development of the adoration of images, purgatory, and transubstantiation are twisting religious values and keeping the common man in darkness. Your smoothness in persuading them to adopt the rituals has been delightfully nefarious and absolutely hellish in its results. In truth, you now have more Christians concerned about purgatory than about Christ!

"Arius, the presbyter of Alexandria, was brilliant in developing our doctrine that Christ, though higher than the human nature, was inferior to God and not eternal. Being in such a powerful political position, many in the upper classes took hold of this idea, even the son and successor of Constantine. Had it not been for that wretch, Athanasius, a puny deacon from Alexandria, we would have turned the church upside down."

"You can call him puny if you want," challenged Nahash, "but we drove him into exile five times and he never wavered. David did not appear like much before our big shot Goliath, either. You haven't forgotten have you?"

Lucifer despised being challenged at all, let alone before the entire demon host. Nahash would surely pay his dues for this insult. Lucifer calmed and continued, "Athanasius, I agree, was the church's champion and a giant in the land. He did whip our man and set back our advance, but Arius did take a good number with him and his teaching will live on!"

"Apollinarius, the bishop of Laodicea who was found leaning our way, served us well also. He asserted our teaching that the divine nature took the place of the human nature in Christ; that Christ was not truly a man, but God alone in a phantom human form. Brilliantly done and another distraction. And then the Pelagius and Augustine battle over an inherited sinful nature, freedom of the human will, and divine election—the church will never agree on that one. Bravo! to all involved. As long as the church is fighting within we have little to worry over.

"Rasha, your work of buttressing the claims of papal authority in Rome were overwhelming. The forging of documents with the signatures of Constantine and early bishops of Rome from the apostles downward, have given rise to a highwater mark of power in Pope Innocent III. The declaration in his inaugural speech shows our reward for such uncontested forgeries: 'The successor of St. Peter stands midway between God and man; below God, above man; Judge of all, judge of none.' Well done, demon host, well done!"

Lucifer paused and surveyed the great assembled throng.

"In short, you have performed with satanic efficiency in destroying and distorting the religion of God. Whatever remnants survive will feel the cruelest punishment we can contrive. With renewed vigor we will have them tortured, beheaded, sawn in half and burned at the stake."

"What have we been doing?" Gonev grumbled to Raa, who nodded grimly.

Lucifer overlooked the exchange and flashed an angry glance.

"We will," he announced, "concentrate first on Christians,

and put satanic fear in the hearts of all who even ponder Christianity. But," he went on, looking straight at Gonev, "our greater weapons will be reason and ridicule. We will adapt our techniques to each class, as we argue with the intellectuals and deride the unthinking masses. We will then dilute their faith and cause them to distort the Word of God with the reason of man.

"As we anticipated from Daniel's prophecy, Rome was overwhelmed by ten nations. We must now, more than ever, take charge of these barbarians, dealing with their families as we did with Greece and Rome before them. You know well that every nation which is careless of its children and its marriage vows destroys itself. We will continue to engineer this destruction.

"At the same time, we must unite in defying the nefarious decree that no world empires will arise after Rome. We will unite and uproot until we establish our own unchallenged world empire, eventually mixing our chosen nations by marriage until they unite under one flag to dominate the world.

"It is crucial that we throw the remnants of Christianity into disarray. We shall, for example, deny Christ's divinity even more than ever before. Distort the Scriptures; cause individuals to shape their doctrines around isolated texts and to ignore the total impact of the Bible. Continue to create many religions. Give them all a piece of the truth, but not enough to lead them to saving faith in Christ. Be sure to allow them the golden rule. This is too basic to deny them anyway, but it is also easy to pervert. Teach them that such a rule is true so long as it does not interfere with their own religious freedom or their sports. But if it counters their beliefs or their personal advancement, teach them how to twist it; that in business and sports any action is fair in their own defense or desire to win; the end justifies the means.

"Keep confusing their languages. The Deity did it at Babel; we will do it our own way now. Give words double meanings, so that once innocent phrases bring a giggle, raise eyebrows or lustful thoughts. So infiltrate language with filth and sexual allusions that they become acceptable even to God's people. For many, especially the intellectuals, cloak frivolity and immorality with sophistication, and in due time they will be leaders of licentiousness. The ruling classes will still be models for the masses, just as the man as head of the home has become the first example in fornication.

"Keep the people in ignorance about the basic *whys* of their actions. Don't let them think things through for themselves. Our continued goal is the fall of man. Every person. Don't forget it. There is none so pitiful and confused as the one who has erred and does not know it. There is no one so low as the person who pretends he is good when he has fallen. But insure that he never turns back to God or you may lose him forever. If, perchance, he somehow returns to God, be sure that he looks back and contemplates the dregs of his fall. Lay guilt upon him until it blocks his view of Christ. Make him feel unworthy, even worthless, and fill him with doubts of his salvation.

"We have done an exhausting work of counterfeiting the Church of God. I speak of your genius in dividing the world into a variety of faiths each believing that the others are anti-God. Many," he laughed, "are ready even to kill to wipe out 'the Godless.' And these 'Godly' conflicts have stirred our bloodiest wars." Laughter and applause rang through the assembly.

"Ariun," he looked at his most cunning demon, "I am pleased with your masterful substitution of the ethics of Confucianism for the righteousness of Christ. Of course, no matter how great the effort, no one could consistently achieve these noble filial and virtuous principles of *Ju* without the help of a higher power. But the oriental leaders made a great pretense. By encouraging their infatuation with this Confucius for idealism's sake, you astutely kept their minds away form the immortality promised by Christ. Absolutely devilish!"

Ariun replied with a squinted smile from his eyes.

"And Nahash, you old serpent," Lucifer grinned, "you likewise did well with Tao—teaching its adherents to abstain from all striving. Their concentration on meditation without allegiance to Christ is a diabolically effective tool. We will carry it into other oriental religions and even into the Christian Church. Anything you can do to preoccupy them, to make them introspective or even to do good without thought of God's glory will lead them from His grasping Hand.

"Yet one of your greatest of all efforts has been with the children of Ishmael—the abandoned children of Abraham. You have comforted them with the prophecies of Mohammed. These single-minded and conscientious people obviously have something to be angry about. Continue to harass them until they are intolerant of all other religions, particularly that of their half-blood brothers, the Jews." His hawklike eyes scanned the room, falling upon a sly-appearing demon.

"You, Ariun, you are good at this type of assignment. I charge you to give them a fanatic zeal, until they will readily die for their god." He threw back his head and laughed.

Ariun sat tall and smiled.

"And lead them to extravagant efforts at proselytizing, if possible, all over the world. As Abraham's descendants they have a logical place in the plan of God, but they are among our most potent agencies to scramble the forces of Christians and to destroy the Jews. In fact, Laylah, I want your dark forces to so agitate the Christians that they will crusade against the sons of Mohammed."

Laylah nodded.

"Needless to say, your smoothness in persuading the Christian Church to adopt the rituals of our pagan gods has been delightfully nefarious and absolutely hellish in its results. In truth, you now have more Christians concerned about purgatory than about Christ. For centuries you have seductively turned the real loyalties of the people to gods of our invention.

"But I have observed that as we tempt and try those who are close to God, they rigidly resist even unto death; our spilling of their blood is scattering their seed on fertile ground. We should have learned this, beginning with the apostles and continuing until recent years."

"How," challenged Rasha, "do you propose that we learn?"

Lucifer paused, but his agitation did not overcome his control.

"Some of you are still too obvious in your rancor. You must step softly, move stealthily, and keep your weapons masked lest you arouse the best candidates for our kingdom from their lethargy. In your persecution make certain that your arguments appear so logical that following the real Christ is perceived as a crime. It is our best remaining way to spit in the face of God. Remember, we are demons without a kingdom. But we dare not rest until we have spoiled every corner of God's creation.

"Consider the way I work," he proclaimed. "Take away a man's self-direction—his will to strive, to help and to heal. A sense of self-worth is among our most dreaded enemies. This is particularly true if man realizes his value as a child of God. So, destroy self-respect and you will destroy the man. Becloud God-given goals, deprive men of confidence and motivation, and they will lose their direction in life and come under our control. Don't be content to control a hundred or ten thousand," he pealed, "but make your goal every one of earth's children."

Lucifer stood taller, pausing with new emphasis. "We have had things going our way since our change of strategy with Constantine. Who would have ever dreamed that the purity of the early church could come to resemble what it is today? Nevertheless, this is not our hour to be drunk with success. Beware of being caught off guard! Something is coming—I can feel it! I fear that if only a few are restored to the enemy's standards, we will have an epidemic of desertion from our ranks. The only way to stop it is to destroy it before it gets roots!

"My command is to kill every traitor from the ranks of our faithful. Is that understood?" Lucifer screamed.

All in the theater rose in affirmation and in strength. No insurrection would get by them.

19
RENAISSANCE AND REFORMATION

In the panorama before us, Lucifer's officers carried on noisily with random conversations. He had to speak out three times before he could command their attention. Since the Messiah, they had become increasingly unstable and often showed their master less respect than in their earlier days. Nevertheless, Lucifer decided this time to ingratiate more than to admonish.

"Greetings," he began, "in the name of satanic defiance of God."

The demons applauded and shouted, "Yea! Yea!"

"The years have been fruitful, and you have performed magnificently. Recent centuries have been among our most productive, and your manipulation of religion has brought a symphony of sorrow to the Deity. Certainly your toying with forms of worship has made religion much more pleasant for man. I am pleased at your widsom and fiendish industry."

The demons nodded to each other with approval.

"The papal crusades against the Moslems of the Holy Land delighted my appetite for retribution against the Most High. Not only did they disturb the Islamic world, but their swords also made their Christian brothers' blood flow." He grinned broadly. "Those Christian Crusaders blatantly denied the meek and quiet spirit of the One they claimed to follow.

"The papal inquisitions were notorious; they will live on among our darkest and most despotic machinations. Your balance of the church and the state in this plague of torture was enormously satisfying to me. When one grew reluctant, you led the other in with fire and sword. Your dedication to this murderous task was especially apparent in Spain. The captivation of King Ferdinand and Queen Isabella in the name of Christ gave the Spanish Inquisition the early force so crucial in such pogroms.

"But," Lucifer turned suddenly serious, "do not let your reckless anger and efforts to please me outdo your true satanic sense. You almost caught St. Ignatius of Loyola in your assassin's net and this would have been unwise. I remind you also that you have been unable to destroy the Waldensian sect."

The multitude squirmed under his hawklike gaze. They remembered forbidden Bibles baked in loaves of bread and bands of Waldensian men defeating small armies in their mountain hideaways.

Lucifer clicked off their triumphs and defeats. "Very clever, the way you have interpolated obscenities into the writings of the poets and the canvasses of the painters. Yet you are permitting a spiritual and cultural Renaissance which I cannot abide."

We could clearly see the flush in Nabal's neck and cheeks. The big chief of staff half turned to Raa and muttered something fiercely out of the corner of his mouth.

Lucifer did not notice. "You have," he hissed, "seen that Huss was burned at the stake, but Luther, who is a much greater threat, has eluded and abashed you at every turn! And Calvin has embarrassed me as explicitly as he has the Pope. You must reach deep within yourselves to use every ounce of hatred that you possess against the servants of our enemy." He again stabbed at the podium. "God protects them. As with old Job, He limits our depredations.

"For millenniums we have successfully peddled the doctrine of righteousness by works—in synagogue, church and pagan grove. Now comes this Martin Luther declaring that the just shall live by faith in Christ alone."

He gnashed his teeth. His high officers slumped deeper in their seats—all except Lashan and Rasha and Raa, who were doing some gnashing of their own.

"I do not want you to be impulsive!" Lucifer shouted; "in fact, I forbid it. But I order you to take every precaution and deviant effort to stop the spread of this gospel of grace which Luther so loudly hails. Our very lives are at stake!"

He hesitated for the sheerest moment. Raa and Rasha had just nudged Lashan who was sitting between them.

He instantly challenged Lucifer. "At what stake?" Lashan inquired coolly and deliberately.

Lucifer was stunned.

"Is there anything *we* can do to save *our* lives?" Lashan penetrated Lucifer's facade almost gleefully.

The audience slumped lower, but obviously enjoyed the exchange. The master began to respond, then decided to ignore "the tongue."

He spoke slowly, word by word, and lowering his voice in an effort to present a picture of composure. "It is imperative that you interrupt man's communication with God. The Reformation is far too advanced now to be totally stolen from the common believer. They have succeeded in making religion conform to Scripture, and the translations into the languages of the nations is very grievous. People are thinking again and religion is once again rooted in personal experience. These are frightening days!

"We must pursue a course of division among these different Protestant groups. Work must accelerate in making each theological difference a major point of separation. These groups must never be allowed to join hands, except when it is in our best interest. Drive them even to take up arms against each other in the name of the enemy. Then we are assured of controlling their influence.

"Wherever the Roman church is still strong, continue our ancient methods of extermination of all those who refuse to conform. Give it a fresh name; call it the 'Counter-Reformation.' For those of you over Spain, France and the Low Countries, I guarantee you great spoils for your efficiency in holding the lines against the insurrection. You will be remembered for some of our darkest and most despotic machinations. Your dedication to this murderous task has already shown itself in Spain. Heat up the flames and sharpen the swords of butchery—tens of thousands will fall at your feet!

"Another move toward the future will be to thrust the Jesuits out to the conversion of as many new nations as possible before the Reformation people get off the ground. South America and Mexico, India, and Canada are ready. Make sure those that go take the Roman gospel! We can afford no more slip-ups.

"There is even talk among the heretics of England and Holland of establishing 'a new world' across the seas. They envision a peaceful lamblike nation where everyone has freedom to worship God as he chooses." He paused.

"Take care how you approach this threat," he admonished. "First, allow the oppressed to seek the new world. As the years pass and its population grows, we will induce other nations to rely on it. Then we will turn it to our ends by defiling its principles. At first it will be necessary to permit it to be a land of freedom. This will be difficult, for the very nature of man—our nature—is intolerant. But we will seek to transform it into a devouring dragon, an oppressive nation."

He now spoke in carefully measured words and tones. "Ominous times are just ahead for us. Lashan is right. There may not be another millennium for us to work. There is a shifting among nations, and there is a significant massing of the forces of our enemy. We must find and exploit every weakness. I have said little about the Renaissance—another of our failures—but I do feel it holds the greatest promise for our handiwork.

"I mentioned your success in interpolating obscenities into the writings of the poets and the canvasses of the painters. Continue to convey an effeminate Christ through art, literature or any other device; carry this concept into the church itself. Pollute the clergy wherever you can. Magnify suspicions about their celibacy, and reason with the priest that they may as well indulge in fornication and perversion because they will be accused anyway.

"We are far behind schedule in forming a world power to follow Rome." He rubbed his large hands across his face in a worried gesture. "I am determined to defy God in this matter," he declared. "Yet more than a thousand years have passed since that iron power fell to the barbarian tribes. The royalty of Europe and the Near East have intermarried, but those nations are still as far from unity as they were a millennium ago. Therefore I have a new proposal to present to you."

The vast audience bent forward in anxious curiosity.

"For centuries we have been successful in destroying the Law of God among all but a few. We must now demolish it among all as a set of principles for human living—to annihilate God's character as the model for man."

Raa was about to ask how he expected to do that when Lucifer glanced his way knowingly. "We will," he said, "subordinate the mysteries of life to human reason. Reason is what this Renaissance is all about and herein lies our weapon. I plan an intense campaign to convince man that God—as a person—does not exist at all. Then I will be their god. The ego of man always waits to be inflated; that provides us a broad avenue to our goal. We will appeal to human reason, without the Spirit of God."

"Just where does he expect to begin?" whispered Rasha to Lashan and Raa.

Lucifer went on as if he heard them well. "The French Empire. Its leaders' obsession with pomp and royal pageantry, and its preoccupation with sensual amusements and violent sports, provides a climate favorable to our most ghoulish ends."

He smiled, enjoying their obvious anticipation. "By distorting the intellectuals' search for truth, we can make reason their altar instead of their pathway. And," he grinned ominously, "the masses will follow them like moths to the fire."

Heads nodded. Even Rasha, Lashan and Raa smiled readily.

"Let us," prophesied Lucifer confidently, "substitute an age of science and technology for the Reformation and give men a new kind of truth. First, suggest to the people that they must be tired of the oppressive hierarchy of the church."

There was now a brief applause.

"Gradually but surely we will attempt to make God the object of man's bitter hatred. By blaming God for their problems, they can be made to deny His existence in the same breath.

And we will carry this obsession with reason and with inventions of men to the end of time. We must not only plague the Roman church, but above all we must undermine the faith of those Bible-quoting Protestants."

Again there was a flurry of applause.

"And it is time to make deeper inroads into art and literature. Man's reason will provide a variety of theories which counter the scriptural story of God's creation of the earth. What we have in the past done indirectly by circumventing God's laws and creating substitute gods, we can now do more directly by intriguing the minds of men with the worship of God in nature—not only the sun and moon and the constellations, but also the birds, beasts and trees. This new pantheism, using only the attribute of God as an all-pervading spirit inhabiting them all, will provide a base for a myriad of rationales that point away from a personal redemptive Christ. Among them will be the theory that life was spontaneous, needing no personal Designer, Planner or Creator. We will convey the notion that higher creatures evolved from lower species who in turn developed from those yet lower, over eons of time. Then we can mesh this theory of evolution with an array of scientific 'findings,' absorbing man's imagination and making the Bible record of creation appear absurd."

Heads jerked up at this last proclamation, and Lucifer's eyebrows arched. "Raa, Lashan, Midbar—do you doubt my word?"

They shifted uneasily, but did not reply.

"Rasha, Raa?" He spoke sharply.

"Not exactly," Raa allowed. "It does seem something of a fantasy to dream that even foolish humans would believe that the world, the universe, and their complex bodies evolved from *nothing*." His voice rose on the last word.

Lucifer's reaction was condescending. "You neglect to consider their colossal egos," he warned.

"Perhaps," admitted Raa.

"Listen carefully to me," the master admonished. "We shall lead men to believe that as life evolved from a single molecule, each form building upon another, man is the crowning stage. Many will eagerly grasp this theory, holding it close and enlarging it to their own glory. They will imagine that man still continues to improve and that there is no limit to his potential.

"Then I direct you to close men's minds to thoughts of trust, so they confuse faith with presumption. As they presume upon God without obeying Him, they will then perceive evolution as demanding no faith!

"We must then move on to comfort any remaining Christians with theories that acknowledge God but which picture Him as the agent of evolution."

The demons laughed approvingly, yet doubting that even the most ignorant of earth's children would believe such a fantasy.

"This plan becomes particularly crucial now with the invention of movable type and the increasing numbers of the Scriptures being issued from the presses. To counter these Bibles, you are to influence the world's editors, printers and writers to produce attractive and seductive literature. Pseudo-scientific tomes and obscenities will be cherished by the leading thinkers.

"While perverting the story of creation, we dare not neglect our continuing assault upon man's stewardship to his God. The more greedy and self-centered he is, the less centered he will be on Deity. The age of reason will become the age of materialism. Where a few previously have seized silver and gold, we will now pervade the whole of mankind with a lust for wealth and make him rebel if he does not possess it."

Lashan, Rasha and Raa had now become deeply thoughtful.

"And," Lucifer continued, "whether they seek the signs of prosperity or the turn of the weather, the outcomes of wars or the champions of sports, whether they want to know future events or need miracles of healing," he now spoke slowly and with great emphasis, "do not forget the power we hold over people through astrology and the occult. I care not what method you use—lying, counterfeit, impersonation—I only charge you to so grip their fears and imaginations that they give up the hope of heaven. Make spiritualism, horoscopy, and other deviltries so urgent and real to them that they find faith too ethereal."

Then Lucifer rose on his toes and stiffened: "What is our business?" he shouted.

"Destruction!" It seemed as if millions of voices were shouting back.

Lucifer's face contorted, a mask of hatred. "Never allow yourselves to become infatuated with your prey no matter how pathetic or fascinating. And never entertain the idea that *you* have any liberty whatsoever, except to do as I command. For most of two thousand years now—since the death and resurrection of Christ—I have perceived doubts among some of you about your course."

His knuckles rapped on the desk. His audience now bent forward in their seats.

"Cherish no illusions; the die is cast. Your only course is to do exactly as I tell you and to be thankful that it is not God you have to obey."

He paused, expectant, waiting their applause. But the applause did not come. They seemed paralyzed. Lucifer remained unmoved. He was too intent on his message.

"And another reminder," he barked. "As princes of liars, murderers, thieves and anarchists, you know the utter satisfaction of creating ruin and desolation. Also," and now again he spoke deliberately, "bear ever in your minds our overriding dedication to the weakening—and eventually the oblivion—of the family. We have shown through Solomon and Belshazzar, Alexander and Nero that the man who cannot manage his own life cannot long lead a nation. And through such as Daniel and Cyrus the Great, the Godhead has shown that the most secure leaders are those who were given warm care and discipline in their youth.

"So, I adjure you to destroy the family. Let no one rest unharmed who cares about the eternal value of his kin."

Without a backward glance, he turned and strode out.

20
THE NEW AGE

Lucifer raised his hand against a roaring applause. "Tonight I have many things to say, so I ask you to stay your applause and listen intently."

He gripped the podium, his knuckles white from strain.

"First, I reassure you of my utter pride over your achievements through the centuries. But we must work ten times harder than ever before to embarrass God before His universe.

"We are faced with a highly organized and awesomely powerful evangelistic force obviously directed by Christ himself." Lucifer spat out the words. "The scattered ashes of Huss and Jerome have grown like prolific seed and have inspired millions against us. Those like Luther and Calvin tore us until we bled from head to foot. The Wesley brothers and their kind have made our wounds deeper, and Dwight Moody is destroying us. Their gospel of mercy and grace hurts us more than threats of hellfire. They are winning converts by the thousands and influencing millions. And now missionaries are going all over the world! These children of God are using the same means of communication and transportation to carry their nefarious gospel that we planned for our own use."

His voice came low and slowly as he paced back and forth across the stage. "My objective now is to deride the Golden Rule, to abolish it as a law of life. I propose, for instance, to prove absurd Christ's teaching to love one's enemies. St. Paul already damaged our cause by teaching brotherly love 'in honor preferring one another.' This gospel is anathema to me.

"I can think of no more alluring way to pervert this principle than to addict Christians to sports. Remember the games of ancient Greece and the gladiators of Rome. They may rationalize in their hypocrisy, but more often, athletes fight to the finish to win for themselves—for their own honor, hardly that of their brothers."

He grinned. "We will encourage their fanatical followers to trail them like pilgrims to a shrine—screaming and applauding themselves into frenzies."

"As you know," he continued, "it is impossible to honor above themselves those brothers they are battling in the arena. But mark my word, they will be so fascinated by their sports that they will rationalize themselves away from the work of Christ and His kingdom. And their followers will spend so much time watching them perform that they will have little time left for God's work."

Raa and Ariun and Midbar were especially obvious in their approval. Lucifer noticed and was pleased. He was determined to destroy free enterprise.

"As daily living becomes easier, all—especially the youth—will be inclined more to play than to work. We must destroy the concept of labor as a builder of responsibility, industry and order. Instead we will build deceit and rivalry, destroying their integrity. The more we laud play and question the nobility of work, the more we will devastate the value systems of society. We will cripple their productivity and distract man from God.

"And we will carry this rivalry into politics, the factory, and even the classroom. We will turn healthy competition into a black-hearted rivalry for honors in which individuals compare themselves among themselves instead of setting principled goals for all. We will so weave this fabric with malice, favoritism and political chicanery that it will bear the hallmark of achievement and become a currency for success."

It was quite clear now to Lucifer that his demons liked this message. It seemed more possible to achieve than some they had heard before.

He squared his great shoulders. "To weaken further the work

ethic, we will use the factories crammed with men, women and youth, to pit the employee against the employer. Wherever possible we will fill the employer with cruelty and greed. Then we can inflame the employee to overreact until wars are fought between capital and labor. This will reduce productivity and self-respect until the nations gasp for their very economic and moral lives. And then we will wipe them out by famine, war or lost freedom.

"Continue to bewilder the family incessantly, to divide and ultimately destroy it. Particularly in industrial societies concentrate on the children. When the men go to war, the women will have to work and relegate their children to the care of others. When the men return, see that the women demand the same license as their husbands. They will be glad to let others care for their children.

"Get the young ones into nurseries, schools, camps—anything to put them out of the security of the home. And make parents unfit to care for their young. As this destroys family life, use these results as even greater justification for children to turn against old family ideals. As the women feel less needed in the home, they will be vulnerable to pressures to work out of the home. Our goal is to capture the children. They are the parents of new generations. Make them become so dependent on peer pressure that they will lose family values and self-direction. Thus when they have families of their own, they will have no values to pass on to them. This is one of our sharpest tools to tear the human race to shreds, and sear the design of God."

Lucifer had by now stimulated an unearthly gleam in the demons' eyes.

"Let man search for self-worth," he said, "but never let him find it. Keep him so skeptical or ignorant of God that he will be indifferent to the Deity's plan to make believers His heirs to share their kingdom. Spoil him with psychological devices to divert him from surrendering totally to the Father.

"Let him think positively, but only of himself. Begin this in childhood, as I admonished you in the times of Israel's kings. Feed the young's fancy with myths and fairy tales at the expense of truth. Soil them with the social contagion of their peers—habits, manners and ridicule. Suggest that only the strong and outwardly beautiful get ahead in the world, accentuating it in the lives of the rich. Since the rich already have everything, focus on wealth at any cost."

Gonev, the "stealer," laughed and agreed out loud, "Yes, at any cost." And his comrades smiled with him.

"Yet," went on Lucifer, "denounce the Bible as the most unlikely of all myths. As I told you before, the theory of evolution would be a heinously disruptive tool. Already we have them convinced that religion and science operate in two separate worlds and never can be connected. Work closely now with scientists to strengthen this theory. Dish out a thousand interpretations of Scripture."

Lucifer glanced over at Ariun, his "cunning" demon, who was almost jumping from his seat in anticipation.

"Suggest that witches, however satanic, are clever and intelligent. Invent saints who appeal to selfishness. Perhaps we will name one Saint Peter or possibly Saint Nicholas."

"Great!" whispered Moot to Nahash. "We could nickname him 'Santa Claus.'"

Lucifer noted the smiles in his leaders, and quickly moved on.

"As new inventions speed up man's lifestyle and the demands of life turn night into day, we will make man even more a creature of the night and so torment his body rhythms that he will think it normal to be nervous and depressed.

"Nabal." He looked down at his chief of staff.

The prince of fools raised his hand in recognition of his master. "Yes?" he asked.

"Nabal, we must accelerate our efforts to induce self-indulgence over principle and common sense, whether in money or food or affairs of the heart. You will lead us in contriving to carry around the world the lewdness of earlier civilizations, multiplying it with the speed of twentieth-century inventions."

Nabal nodded and Lucifer continued. "With this kind of thinking and the behavior it brings, man will fulfill prophecy."

The crowd tittered in anticipation and there was scattered applause.

"The predictions of St. Paul will indeed come true: Man will ever be learning and never able to come to the knowledge of truth."

The crowd roared.

"And as Hosea prophesied, people shall be destroyed for a lack of His knowledge."

There was spontaneous applause and shouts of "Hear! Hear!"

"Once again!" cried Lucifer, buoyed by this reception, "I admonish you to keep man from understanding that God in fact owns everything. Distract him as you would any naughty child. Make him indifferent to God. Especially obscure the command to tithe. See that he returns little or nothing to his Maker—in silver or gold, his children, or even his time. Make him as greedy as you and I."

The demons were jubilant!

"Use a light touch, especially at first, and he will follow like lambs follow the Judas goat. But don't overdo it! Man is so full of greed since his Eden fall that if you keep him inherently—not grossly, just inherently—self-centered, he must quite logically turn from his Maker. He will naturally reach out for power, and often violence will erupt. In his selfish disposition he will usurp even the authority of God in judging his fellowmen, leading his family, his village and even his nation in insane acts of vengeance for imagined wrongs."

There was now nodding at almost every sentence.

"But you must become particularly skilled in carrying this vengeance into the synagogue, church, and mosque. For those who are determined not to reveal anger, simply see that they are politely resentful. That will be enough to keep them insulated from the Spirit of Christ."

Ariun looked over at Nabal and Raa in the officer group and coolly winked.

"And now," added Lucifer, "it is time to multiply creeds and cults with fiendish delight. We will split, reform, and cultivate offshoots and cults—any contrivance to adulterate the Deity's gospel. We must so insidiously arrange these cults within and among all religious groups that they are almost impossible to distinguish even by the very elect of God. Those who do not intimately know Him and His Word will be caught in our web. For those who are accustomed to church attendance, we will supply a legion of distractions—secret societies, elitist clubs, concerts, festivals, follies and fairs. Preoccupy them not only with culture and science and art, but with every rumor—from the 'adventures' of the Illuminata to fascination with our mysterious flying objects. And so captivate them with commerce and trade and the pressures of survival that they forget they have a God.

"Now more than ever we shall give mankind entré into the darkest sanctums of our most evil environs—to let them use us as we use them!"

Lucifer looked over at Hoshek, his apostle of darkness, and was rewarded with that demon's crafty nod.

"This," said the master, "shall not be as hard to do as it would have been centuries ago. The modern churches are numerous and eager to confuse; many defensively accuse and detract from the others. They talk about unity, but seldom on matters that require sacrifice of their cherished rituals and doctrines. For the most part these groups have now adopted much of our creed. Whether using the Koran, the Torah, the Bible, or other religious guides, they largely interpret these writings for their convenience more than their needs. Their Sabbaths now vary, their perception of the dead is confused, and they are often at astonishing variance from the clearest of scriptural word on the divine outlines for the future. In short, they are ripe for our darkest spiritualistic works."

Lucifer again looked directly at Hoshek and Skahor, his officers of darkness. They grinned broadly and nodded.

"For millenniums now we have used witches and wizards, magicians, and fortunetellers and astrologers. These must now be refined, *every single one*, to fit discreetly into the purest congregations. We have already pervaded much of the Christian Church with the universalist doctrine of the soul's immortality." He smiled, self-satisfied. "Ariun, my friend, what does the belief that everyone who dies enters a new life in heaven teach earth's children?"

The "cunning one" beamed, equal to the question. "We bring death," he asserted, "and by inference, deliverance from the pain and sorrow of earth. It is as if we were in partnership with our old enemy," he chuckled. "God runs heaven and we run earth."

"Well said," Lucifer nodded. "Our version that these creatures go to heaven when they die makes *us* the heroes. It is our delightful duty, you see, to weaken their bodies and cause accidents and epidemics, bringing death to them."

He paused, reflecting. "Amazing, isn't it, how untold numbers have believed our first bit of trickery, 'You will not surely die.'"

His teeth were now clenched, his long finger pointed downward. "The darker and deeper we persuade men to delve into these areas, the more we can control them until they become our most persuasive agents. We will continue to perform our own brand of miracles through them, such as laying on blindness or illness, then removing it with prayers. And performing mysteries through those we designate as saints."

Ariun nudged Gonev, giving him a big grin and nod.

"On the other hand," Lucifer instructed, "continue to make fools of men through magic and voodoo, séances and astrology."

Again there was a notable flurry and agreement among the demons as a number of the officers looked at each other.

"Offer tantrums and fears, nightmares and apparitions, vile thoughts and compulsive acts," Lucifer continued. "Cripple their limbs, give them disease, dizziness, and depression; supply them such birthmarks and warts and skin diseases as to multiply embarrassment and ridicule. Tempt mothers in pregnancy to such addictions as will disfigure their offspring. Then we can perplex social institutions with their care."

His fist slammed the podium. "Now, more than ever before, is the time to harass the God-fearing person—any man, woman, or even the smallest child. Again I adjure you: Oppress them, depress them, and ultimately go into them and possess them. Control their minds, their very words. Never mind the threat of exorcism; rather, popularize it as a fascinating sport. It is not even a gamble, for where you lose one to God, you gain a hundred for me."

He bent forward, shaking a bony finger toward his intensely interested audience.

"Take care," he admonished, "to avoid the prayers of simple Christians who wait for the quiet voice of the Holy Spirit. They may not be as articulate as a Wesley or a Moody, but you will easily know them—those who take in the orphan, clothe the naked, feed the hungry and free the oppressed. Use every distraction to keep them from waiting long on their knees or getting deeper into their Bibles."

Lucifer's face contorted and the admission seemed forced from his lips.

"They make me tremble," he declared.

Rasha and Raa had just that day admitted that they were underestimating the "little men." Lucifer took note of their apparent agreement and gave a momentary signal of this pleasure. Then he went on.

"It is this kind of person whose faith must be aborted *before* he fully experiments with God." He heavily emphasized "before."

"Flatter him, discourage him, prosper him, or worry him," he commanded. "Turn his eyes on the failures of the clergy, tempt him to doubt, do anything to turn him even from his Maker. If he has any position within the church, such as deacon or preacher, appeal to his vanity. Teach ministers to depend more upon voice and diction and theology than on a humble love for their brothers. Insure that their sermons rely more on tradition, heartless commentaries and the approval of their human peers than upon the Holy Spirit and the work of God."

Now Lucifer clasped his great hands and leaned gravely over the podium.

"I will personally take the lead," he vowed, "in this great final deception and disruption."

"When hasn't he?" breathed Lashan as Lucifer spoke on.

"My goal is to make ineffective the words of the prophets. Whether ancient or modern, we will favor none; instead, bringing up new seers at every hand. False prophets will be among our keenest tools. Let their words remain close to the line of God. They need depart from God's Word only an iota, and the children of God will be confused. So I will personally—and discreetly—lead them to veer ever so slightly from the Scriptures."

Lucifer now seemed very sure of himself.

"Meanwhile," he added, "it is imperative that you keep earth's children so busy with amusements, sports, and the cares of their daily lives that they do not have time to study deeply the Word of God. Again I adjure you to see that they attempt the work of God in their own power. Humanism must reign!"

"That's the way," agreed Ariun. "Keep them distracted from God."

"Yes," nodded Gonev, "distraction is the key." They listened intently as Lucifer spoke with increasing power.

"You know well by now that the only test to determine truth is precisely what the Scriptures say: 'To the law and to the testimony: if they speak not according to this word . . . there is no light in them.' So keep all the people—but especially ministers—from immersion in the writings of God. Let them quote. Let them excerpt. But keep them from total devotion to the prophecies and instructions of God."

There was a scattering of applause.

"We do not care if it is only to ignore Him on little things—the illogical things, the impractical things. We must see that in their intellectual egotism they find a thousand reasons to put aside the words of the prophets, old and new. When we convince them to view the Scriptures as unlikely or impossible, ignoring them as not of God, then we can confuse them, convincing them that the tragedies which we arrange—handicap, disease, injury and death—are actually the work of an angry God."

He waited, arms clasped overhead, for the applause and shouts of approval.

"Remember," he added slowly and with finality, "you and I were once ministers of God in this universe."

His mouth opened; he hesitated, clearing his throat. "We must face reality."

Every eye was sharply upon him, every ear alert.

"We are condemned to die. No one but the Deity perceives

the tortures that await us when God withdraws His protection, destroying us by His glory." His voice broke; for an instant it seemed he would choke, but he clutched the podium with both hands, then straightened.

"Yet in closing this meeting I suggest that to meditate on such a fate is not the most comforting way to deal with the future. I propose that we become so utterly consumed in our work of seduction and death that we begrudge even a moment to ponder the wrath of God. From this moment on I will employ every ounce of my energy to multiply my efficiency and reach my hellish goals."

His hawklike gaze swept the entire assembly.

"I will never concede defeat!" he raved. "What say you?"

As one body his servants arose, cheering hysterically. Lucifer raised his clasped hands in a final, incongruous signal of victory before striding away.

The rest of the story is now being filmed, and you are among the actors.